Allyn and Bacon
Quick Guide to the Internet
for Education

Allyn and Bacon

Quick Guide to the Internet
for
Education

1998 Edition

Joseph D. Rivard

Central Michigan University

Allyn and Bacon
Boston • London • Toronto • Sydney • Tokyo • Singapore

Copyright © 1998 by Allyn and Bacon
A Viacom Company
160 Gould Street
Needham Heights, Massachusetts 02194

Internet: www.abacon.com
America Online: keyword: College Online

ISBN 0-205-27929-5

Printed in the United States of America

10 9 8 7 6 5 4 3 2   01 00 99 98 97

Contents

Get Connected Now!

Load, click and cruise on the Internet with Sprint Internet Passport (SM) for news, information, entertainment and much more. With Sprint Internet Passport, you get full-service, direct Internet access from Sprint, friendly customer service support on-line or by phone 24 hours a day, seven days a week. You'll be able to easily browse around the World Wide Web, and you'll also receive one E-mail account for communicating with family, friends and colleagues. In addition when you get connected with Sprint Internet Passport, you'll receive full access to more than 18,000 Usenet newsgroups, local service from more than 200 U.S. cities (more planned in 1997) and reliable service from one of the Internet's largest carriers.

Pricing for Sprint Internet Passport is $19.95 a month for unlimited use,* or you can pay only for the hours you use at a rate of $1.50 per hour. For your convenience, we'll bill your VISA®, MasterCard® or American Express®.

Just double click on the Sprint icon to start your Internet experience.

Sprint Installation Instructions

DO NOT INSTALL SOFTWARE until you have read the Software License agreement which appears on the CD.

If you currently use Netscape® Navigator as your Internet browser, Sprint Internet Passport will automatically overwrite that software. However, with just a little extra care and effort, Sprint Internet Passport will nicely coexist on your system with your current software. More information and details on the exact steps necessary to preserve your current configuration can be found at http://www.sprint.com/passport, or you can call us at 1-800-786-1400.

---

*Nation-wide 800 access number includes surcharge of $4.80 per hour if local service is not available in your area.

Windows® 3.1 Users

1. Insert the *Sprint Internet Passport* installation CD into your CD-ROM drive.

2. In *Program Manager* or *File Manager,* select *File* from the menu bar, and then select Run.

3. In the *Command Line* field, type *D:\INSTALL* (where D: represents the drive letter of your CD-ROM).

4. Click *OK,* then follow the on-screen prompts to complete the software setup. When you're prompted to do so, allow setup to restart Windows®.

5. When restart is complete, double-click on the *Sprint Internet Passport Account Setup* icon in the *Sprint Internet Passport* program group.

6. Follow the on-screen prompts to set up your *Sprint Internet Passport* account.

7. When registration is completed, double-click on the *Sprint Internet Passport* icon in the *Sprint Internet Passport* program group.

8. Click *Dial.*

You're ready to begin!

Windows95® Users

1. If you have never been on-line before, be sure to have your Windows95® diskettes or *Sprint Internet Passport* CD handy.

2. Insert the *Sprint Internet Passport* installation CD into your CD-ROM drive. On most systems, the setup process will begin automatically within about 10 seconds.

3. If the setup program doesn't begin automatically, click the *Start* button on your Task Bar and then click *Run.* In the *Run* window, type *D:\INSTALL* (where *D:* represents the drive letter of your CD-ROM) and click *OK.*

4. Follow the on-screen prompts to complete the software setup. If you're prompted for a Windows95® diskette, place the required diskette in *Drive A:;* if you're prompted for the Windows95® CD, remove the *Sprint Internet Passport* CD from your CD-ROM drive and insert your Windows95® CD. If you're prompted to do so, allow set up to restart your computer.

5. Double-click the *Sprint Internet Passport Account Setup* icon in the *Navigator* window.

6. Follow the on-screen prompts to set up your Sprint Internet Passport account.

7. Once registration is completed, double-click on the *Dial Sprint Internet Passport* icon on your desktop to connect to Sprint Internet Services.

8. If the password field is blank (no stars), enter your password.

9. Click Connect.

10. Double-click the *Sprint Internet Passport* icon on your desktop to launch the Sprint Internet Passport Browser (Netscape Navigator).

You're ready to begin!

Macintosh Users

1. Insert the Sprint Internet Passport installation CD into your CD-ROM drive.

2. The *Sprint Internet Passport* window will appear on your desktop. Inside this window, double-click the *Installer* icon.

3. Follow the on-screen prompts to complete the software setup. Be sure to take the default settings. (Note that default settings are outlined in black on your screen.)

4. When setup is complete, you will be prompted to restart your computer. Click on *Restart*.

5. When restart is complete, the Account Setup window appears. Click on the *Next* arrow in the Account Setup window.

6. Follow the on-screen prompts to set up your Sprint Internet Passport account.

   During Account Setup, your computer will attempt to connect to the registration service to open your account. *If you are using Macintosh System 7.1,* you will be prompted to restart your computer. Click on Restart. When restart is complete, the Account Setup window appears. Click on the *Connect Now* arrow to continue with Account Setup.

7. When registration is complete, you will be prompted to restart your computer. Click on *Restart.*

8. When restart is complete, double-click on the *Sprint Internet Passport* icon in the Sprint Internet Passport window. *FreePPP* will connect you to Sprint Internet Services, and the Sprint Internet Passport browser will launch.

You're ready to begin!

Exiting your Sprint Internet Passport Account

If you're using Windows® 3.1

- Close *Sprint Internet Passport (Netscape Navigator)* by clicking on *File* and then clicking on *Exit.*
- Close any other open Internet client applications (e.g., IRC, FTP, and Telnet sessions).
- Disconnect from *Sprint Internet Passport* by clicking the *Disconnect* button in the *Sprint Internet Dialer* box.

If you're using Windows95®

- Close *Sprint Internet Passport (Netscape Navigator)* by clicking on *File* and then clicking on *Exit.*
- A message will come up stating that there are open modem connections. Choose "yes" to disconnect from the Internet.
- Close any other open Internet client applications (e.g., IRC, FTP, and Telnet sessions).

- Check to make sure there is no button on the Task Bar labeled *Connected to Sprint Internet*. If there is, click on it to bring up the *Sprint Dialer Dialogue* box and click on the *Disconnect* button.

If you're using a Macintosh

- Close *Sprint Internet Passport (Netscape Navigator)*.
- Double-click on the FreePPP Setup icon in the Sprint Internet Passport folder.
- Click Disconnect.

Notes

Be sure to record your:

- Dial Access Number
- Sprint Internet Passport Password
- E-mail Address
- Sprint Internet Passport Log-in ID

A README file has been included on your Sprint Internet Passport CD. Windows® 3.X users can find it here: *D:\WIN.31\DISK5\README.TXT* (where D: represents your CD-ROM drive). Windows95® users can access the file by clicking on Start, Clicking on Run, typing *D:\WIN.95\DISK5\README.TXT* (where D: represents your CD-ROM drive), and clicking OK.

For Macintosh users, the *README.txt File* can be found in the Sprint Internet window on the CD.

Your software will automatically search for and attempt to identify your modem. However, if setup encounters difficulties, you may need to identify your modem manually. See the *README.txt File* for more information. Be sure to verify your pricing plan selection.

Be sure your registration address matches your credit card billing address. If your credit card company uses ZIP+4, it is important that you include the extra 4 digits.

If you live in an area where local calls can span two or more area codes, you may want to modify the 1+Area Code settings in your dialer. See the *README.txt File* for more information.

Please review all the numbers available to help ensure your modem dialer is set for a local call. If you are unsure if a number is a local call, check with your local telephone company. Please note that in some areas, a call may be considered long distance, even though it does not require dialing a "1" or "0".

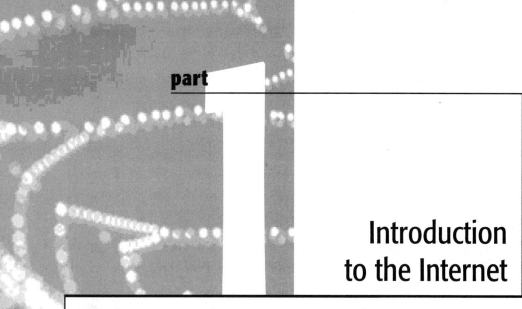

part

1

Introduction
to the Internet

The Internet—Communication in the '90s

The Internet is a loose affiliation of computers and computer networks. These networks range in size from small, one-computer operations of individual users and small businesses to the super-sized networks at large corporations and universities.

Who's in Charge Here?

You can think of the Internet as a kind of United Nations, serving only to facilitate the rules by which information is passed from one member to another. The Internet is nothing more than a few committees who establish the rules and languages by which the computers in the member networks talk to each other. Just as the United Nations does not control what goes on within the member countries, there is no organization called the "Internet" that controls what goes on inside each member network.

The Internet is also international in scope and no single government controls it. On one hand this near anarchy has allowed the Internet to grow at an unbelievable rate, but on the other hand the lack of a governing body means that the Internet is a bit like the old Wild West—anything and everything goes, and there's no sheriff to keep law and order.

The Information Explosion

The proliferation of education-related Websites will be illustrated in the following pages. A single example, the home page of AskERIC, offers not only general information but hyper-link connectors to more specific subjects. "Clicking" on one of the items shown at the bottom of the screen will transfer you to the page which contains the information you are requesting.

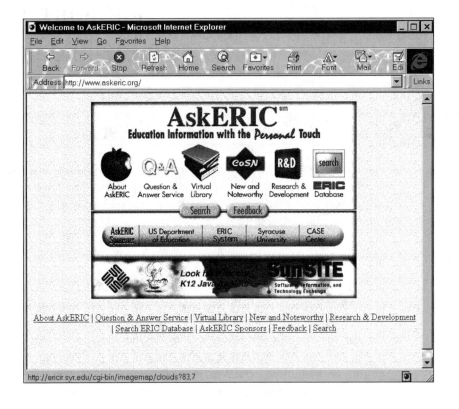

part

1

The AskERIC home page. This page contains a tremendous amount of information on various topics in the field of education. Searching the ERIC database is often one of the first methods students and professionals use to identify research and researchers in specific educational areas.

Significance for Communication, Education, and Research

The Internet provides simultaneous in-depth information to multiple users. This electronic enhancement of knowledge contrasts with a newspaper which can only be read by one person at a time. Below are three Websites which illustrate the wide array of groups, organizations and companies which specialize in educational services. Following these are other Web addresses which will start you on your way.

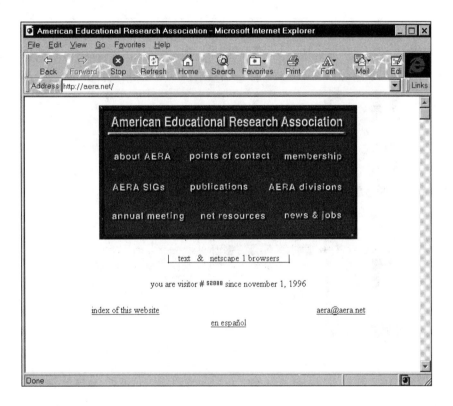

part

1

The American Educational Research Association home page. From action research to education in science and technology, AERA is an organization which provides for the widest array of research interests in the field.

This is the home page for the *Exploratorium* located in the *Palace of Fine Arts* in San Francisco, California. It's an interesting site dealing with science, psychology, and learning as well as many other intriguing topics.

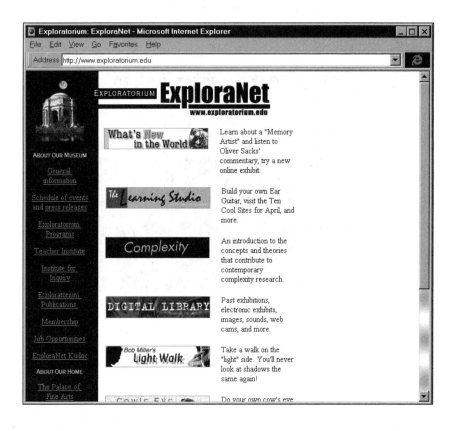

part

1

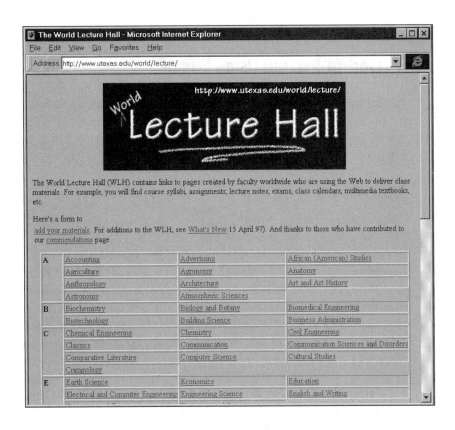

This site is the *World Lecture Hall* at the University of Texas Austin; it contains many interactive links not only to education but to most other disciplines in the university. This site was one of the pioneer sites in developing the Internet as a teaching tool.

Person-To-Person: Using E-mail

Electronic mail, or E-mail, is one of the most important applications of the Internet. E-mail is personal correspondence between individual users, and is the electronic equivalent to the familiar paper-based postal service.

How It Works

Every Internet Service Provider operates a post office 24 hours a day, 365 days per year to receive messages sent to its customers and to forward the mail they send to other people. Messages addressed to you are stored on the post office computer until you are ready to read them.

When you send an E-mail message to another person, you first transmit the message to your provider's post office which starts the message on its way to the post office at the recipient's service provider. Messages are usually passed between several post office computers on their way from one provider to another.

part

1

Personal Addresses on the Internet Each user on the Internet has a unique name. The name is made up of two parts: the user name and the domain name. The user name identifies the individual user, and the domain name identifies the Internet Service Provider.

For example, the E-mail address "psmith@uiuc.edu" is for a user named "P. Smith" at an organization (domain) called "uiuc.edu". The two pieces are always separated by '@'.

All domain names for organizations in the United States end with a three-letter abbreviation which specifies the type of organization. The common abbreviations are:

- .com   a company or business
- .edu   an educational institution
- .net   a commercial Internet service provider
- .org   an organization that is not a business

Domain names from other parts of the world end with a two-letter abbreviation that specifies the country in which the organization is located. For example, "pat_smith@emwac.ed.ac.uk" is for a user named "Pat Smith" at an organization located in the United Kingdom.

Mail Programs

There are many different mail programs available, and they all provide similar functions and use similar terminology. We're going to give example from two popular mail programs: Netscape Mail and Microsoft Internet Mail.

Mail programs organize your messages in areas called *folders*. Typical folders are called **Inbox,** which holds the mail that has been sent to you, **Outbox** which holds mail you have written but not yet sent, and **Sent** which hold copies of messages you have sent to other people. You can also create your own folders as a way to save messages you have received in an organized fashion.

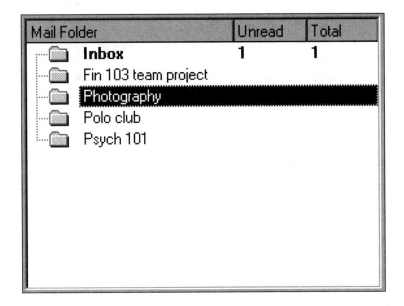

Using folders to organize messages you have received or sent can be a very convenient way to maintain a complete record of an E-mail "conversation."

Sending a Message

In this section we'll go step-by-step through the process of sending an E-mail message to another user. The steps are given for the Netscape Mail and Microsoft Internet Mail programs. If you are using a different mail program consult the program's documentation for complete instructions.

Using Netscape Mail

1. Click the To:Mail button in the toolbar or select the **New Mail Message** option from the **File** menu.

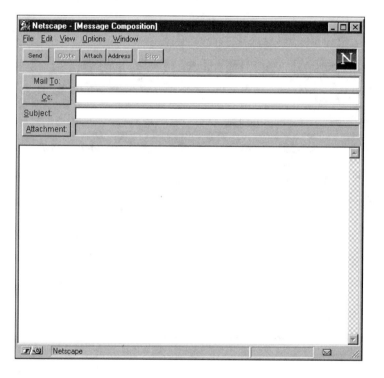

2. Type the recipient's E-mail address on the "Mail To:" line. If you want to send the same message to more than one person, put a semicolon between the E-mail names. You can build up an electronic address book which can be accessed by clicking on the **Mail To:** button.

3. Press TAB to move to the "CC:" line. Type the address of people to whom you would like to send a copy of the message. Don't type anything here if you don't want to send copies or you have already listed everyone on the "To:" line.

part

1

4. Press TAB again and type a subject line for the message.

5. Press TAB again and type the body of your message. When you have finished writing the message, either click the **Send** button or choose the **Send Now** option from the **File** menu.

Using Microsoft Internet Mail

1. Click the **New Message** button in the toolbar or select the **New Message** option from the **Mail** menu.

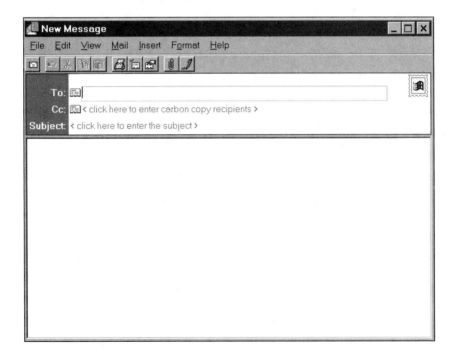

part

1

2. Type the recipient's E-mail address on the "To:" line. If you want to send the same message to more than one person, put a semicolon

between the E-mail names. You can build up an electronic address book which can be accessed by clicking on the file card icon.

3. Press TAB to move to the "CC:" line. Type the address of people to whom you would like to send a copy of the message. Don't type anything here if you don't want to send copies or you have already listed everyone on the "To:" line.

4. Press TAB again and type a subject line for the message.

5. Press TAB again and type the body of your message. When you have finished writing the message, either click the send icon or choose the **Send Message** option from the **File** menu.

Your E-mail message starts it journey to the recipient's system as soon as you press the Send key. Once you send a message there is no way to get it back or stop it from reaching its destination.

Now practice sending a message by sending a message to yourself. Start your mail program and follow the steps listed above.

part
1

■ Type your own E-mail address in the "Mail To:" or "To:" field.

■ Leave the "CC:" field blank.

■ Type "Test Message" on the "Subject line"

■ Type "This is a test message. Did you get it?" for the body of the message. When you're finished use the "Send" option to send the message to yourself.

Reading and Responding to Messages

Using Netscape Mail

1. When you start Netscape Mail, the display shows a list of messages that have been sent to you. Messages that you have not yet read are listed in bold type.

   The "Sender" column shows who send the message, the "Subject" column displays the subject line, and the "Date" column shows the date on which the message was received.

2. The message you just sent to yourself should be listed in the window. Double-click the message line in the listing.

3. The message appears in the lower part of the window.

part

1

Using Microsoft Internet Mail

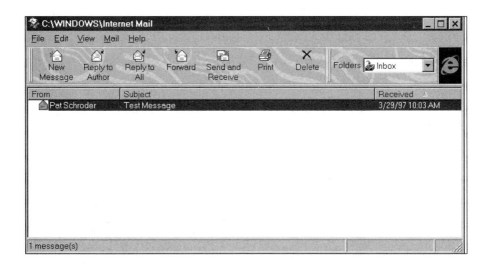

1. When you start Microsoft Internet Mail, the display shows a list of messages that have been sent to you. Messages that you have not yet read are listed in bold type.

   The "From" column shows who send the message, the "Subject" column displays the subject line, and the "Received" column shows the date on which the message was received.

2. The message you just sent to yourself should be listed in the window. Double-click the message line in the listing to open the mail reading window.

3. The message reader pops open and shows you the message.

part

1

After you've read the message you can reply to it, then you can either delete it or file it in a folder for later reference. Using the reply feature of your mail reader is how you carry on an E-mail conversation.

You receive a message that you reply to, then you receive a reply to your reply, you reply to that, and so on.

This kind of E-mail conversation may take place over a period of a few days or weeks; it's sometimes hard to keep the context of the conversation in mind when reading replies. Mail reader programs include a feature called Quoting that copies the message you are replying to and makes it part of your reply. When you use this feature you send back the original message along with your reply. This helps the person reading the reply remember the context of the message.

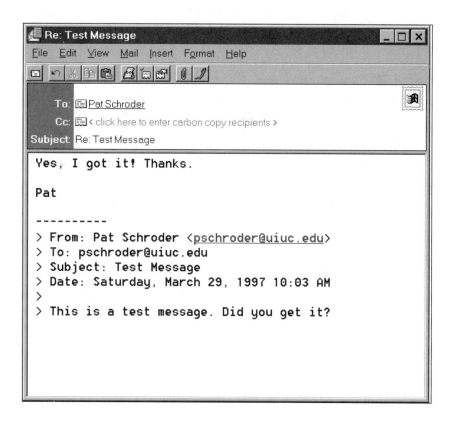

How to Locate Addresses

One major problem with the Internet is that there is no equivalent of the phone book. If you don't know someone's E-mail address there is no way to look them up in a directory. There are a few experimental directory assistance services in development, but so far they cover only a very small fraction of the millions of people who have E-mail addresses.

As you work with the Internet you will find many opportunities to compile an address book of E-mail addresses for future reference. Build up your own address book by watching for addresses on paper-based and electronic documents. Look for addresses on letterheads and other stationary. You should also copy the E-mail addresses from messages you receive. When you start surfing the Web (covered in a later chapter), you will have more opportunities to discover E-mail addresses.

E-mail Etiquette

A set of etiquette rules have been developed over the years to make electronic interactions more pleasant and orderly. You should follow these rules of behavior, sometimes called "netiquette", when using E-mail.

Don't use all upper case. Using upper case letters to emphasize words in your messages is the E-mail equivalent of shouting. It's considered very bad manners to write messages in upper case.

Use emoticons and acronyms. The person reading your messages does not have the benefit of seeing your facial expressions and body language as with a face-to-face encounter. This is a very important limitation of E-mail, and you must always consider how your words might be interpreted. It's very hard for someone to know if you are kidding or are being very serious. *Emoticons* and acronyms have been developed over the years as a way of showing facial expressions or conveying feelings in the text of a message.

An emoticon is a set of characters that represent an emotion or facial expression. Common emoticons you may see in messages are:

: -)	smile
; -)	wink
: - n(	frown
\<g\>	grin
\<vbg\>	very big grin

An acronym is a form of shorthand. The letters of the acronym stand for an expression. Common acronyms in messages are:

AFAIK	as far as I know
IMO	in my opinion

part

1

IMHO	in my humble opinion
BTW	by the way
OTOH	on the other hand
CU	see you

Use emoticons and acronyms in your messages to help convey the subtle (or not-so-subtle) meanings behind your words. It may make a world of difference whether you write "Idiot!<g>" or "Idiot!" to the person reading your message.

Don't quote everything. Although quoting is a convenient way to maintain the context of a series of messages, messages become unreadable if you quote too much or quote a quote that includes a quote. Quote judiciously.

Keep your signature short. Some mail programs allow you to set up a *signature block*. This is a few lines of information that acts as your signature on a mail message. It's best not to put too much information in your signature block; your name and organizational affiliation are enough. You should not put your postal mailing address, phone number, fax number, web site address, and favorite quote in your signature. Signatures should be very short, not longer than the messages they are attached to. Some people pay for E-mail services or have slow connections to the Internet, and this unnecessary information costs them time and money.

part

1

Be polite. Somewhere a researcher is studying the curious phenomenon that people will write things in an E-mail message that they would never say to someone's face. On the Internet, being intentionally rude and insulting is called *flaming* and has become a kind of sport for some people. You can unwittingly become the target of a flame attack by simply making a breach of netiquette in a public forum. If someone sends you an E-mail message calling you a "clueless newbie," you've been flamed.

Many people enjoy flaming newcomers to the net. They will try to insult you because of your lack experience using the net or the incorrect use of Internet terminology. Resist the temptation to reply to a flame attack. A flaming reply to a flame starts what is called a *flame war,* a kind of pointless Internet shouting match that can go on and on forever until one of the participants finally gives in at which point the opponent has "won" the war.

It's one thing to point out a mistake in someone's message, but do it in a polite way and back up your point with facts. A critical response should be more like a debate than a brawl. Don't just send a message saying, "Everyone knows such-and-such, and only a complete idiot and fool would think otherwise." Life's short. Lighten up.

On-Line Discussions: Newsgroups and Listservers

Newsgroups vs. E-mail

E-mail is a great person-to-person communication medium, but it's not very good for large group interaction. If the group consists of more than a few people, adding all the names to the "To:" or "CC:" list gets to be a tedious chore and it's hard to be sure that everyone sees the all of the replies. *Newsgroups* were developed to address this limitation.

A newsgroup is an electronic message board. The message board keeps track of several discussions simultaneously by organizing the messages and replies in groups called *threads*. A thread starts with the original message, or *post,* and includes all of the replies made by every participant in the discussion. You can follow the discussion by reading the thread from beginning to end. This makes it possible for several people to collaborate on a project or continue a discussion over a long period of time.

part

1

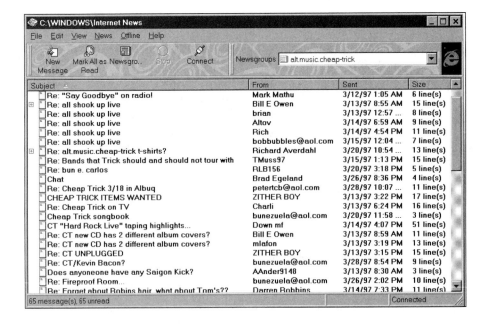

A program called a news reader is used to read newsgroups and follow the threads. News readers operate very much like E-mail programs, but they also provide features that let you follow threads and keep track of your place in several continuing discussions. We'll be looking at the Netscape Navigator News Reader and the Microsoft Internet News programs for examples in this section. Other news readers offer similar services and work in much the same way.

Locating Newsgroups

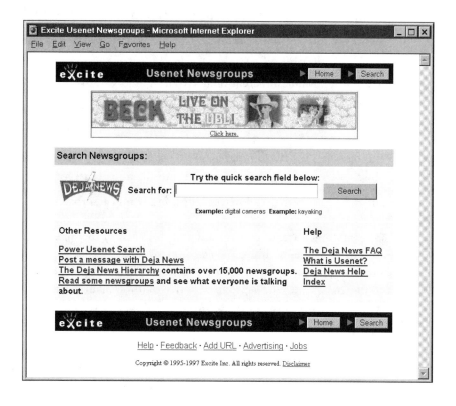

part

1

You can participate in tens of thousands of public and private newsgroups. You are usually invited to join a private newsgroup or find out about it because of your affiliation in an organization or participation in an activity. The discussion topics in a private newsgroup are likely to be very focused.

Your Internet Service Provider will carry as many as 20,000 public newsgroups in which you can participate. Just about every topic you can think of is covered, and a few that may shock and possibly offend you as well. When you hear stories on the news about all the smut and terrible things that are available on the Internet, the reporters are usually talking about newsgroups.

Newsgroups are organized in a hierarchy. There are a small number of main categories, each of which is broken down into subtopics, and further broken down into specific topics of interest. A sampling of the main categories you are likely to encounter includes:

comp	computer science and general computer-related topics
news	newsgroups pertaining to the operation of the Internet newsgroup system
rec	hobbies, recreational activities, and various arts
sci	scientific research, the applications of science and engineering, and some social sciences
soc	social issues
misc	anything that doesn't fit into the above categories
alt	"alternative" newsgroups, many unusual topics

The subtopics are, of course, different for each of the main categories. For example, within the "rec" category there is a subtopic "photo" for photographic-related discussions. This group of topics is called the "rec.photo" newsgroups. Notice that the main category is named first, followed by a period, then the subtopic name. The specific newsgroup dedicated to the discussion of photographing people is called "rec.photo.people".

Listing Newsgroups

The list of newsgroups available to you is downloaded to your computer and kept up to date by the news group reader program. Specific instructions for browsing the newsgroup list depend on the particular newsgroup reader program.

Netscape Navigator News Reader

1. Select the **Show All Newsgroups** from the **Options** menu of Netscape Navigator. The list of available newsgroups is shown in the **News Servers** window. This window is organized like an outline. To locate a newsgroup you have to "expand" the levels of the outline. Click on the '+' sign next to an entry to see the subentries. Keep on clicking '+' signs until you get to the lowest level in the section you are interested in.

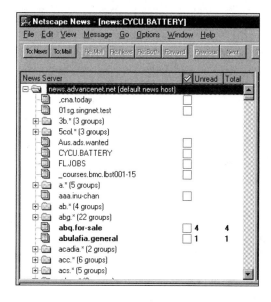

2. Click on the newsgroup name in the Newsgroups box. A list of messages appears in the window.

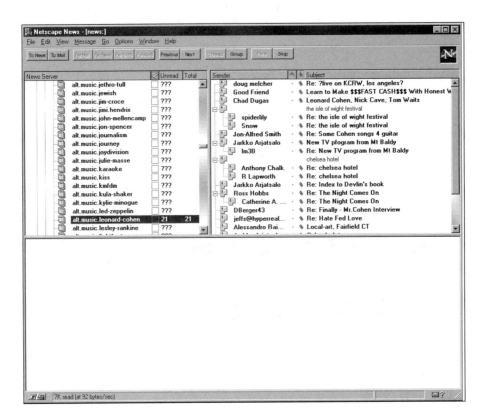

Microsoft Internet News

1. Click the **Newsgroups** button in the toolbar or select the **Newsgroups** option from the **News** menu.

2. Click the **All** tab in the newsgroups window to display the entire list of newsgroups. You can browse the entire list of newsgroups by scrolling the list, or locate a newsgroup by typing a word in the "Display newsgroups which contain" box at the top of the page.

3. Click on the newsgroup name in the Newsgroups box and then click the **Go To** button to immediately see the messages for that newsgroup.

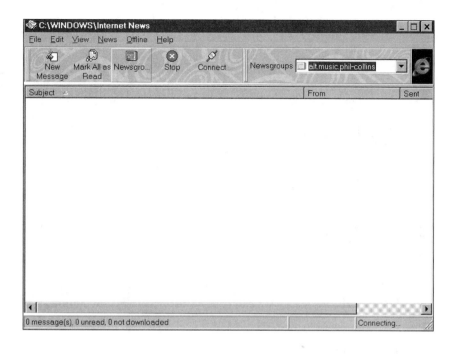

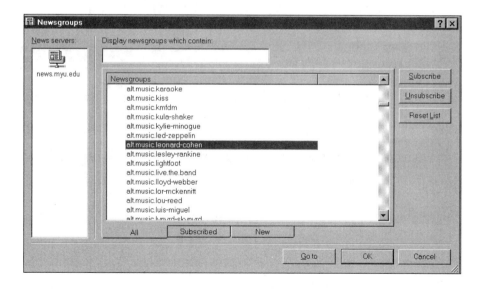

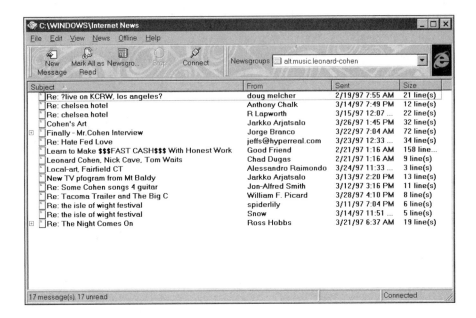

Reading Messages

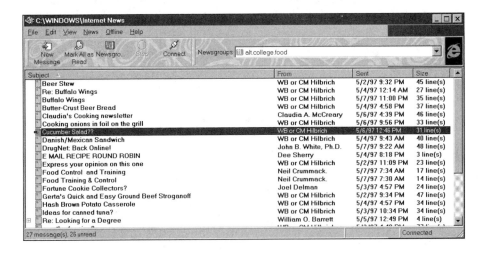

Once you have selected a newsgroup the news reader program displays a list of messages. The title of the message, name of the sender, and the date on which the message was written are displayed. You will often see "Re:" as the first part of the message title. That means "Regarding" and indicates that the message is a reply to a previous message on the same topic. Some news reader software automatically groups the messages by topic. A series of messages on the same topic is called a *thread*.

Double click on the message title line to display the message. The text of the message is displayed in a window.

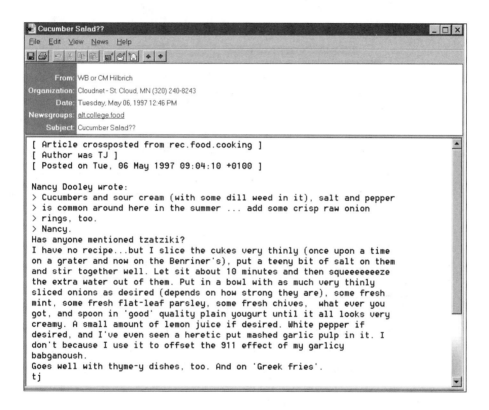

part

1

Once you locate a newsgroup that you are interested in reading, you have two choices. You can subscribe to the news group and let your news reader program keep track of which messages you have already seen, or you can just drop in from time to time and notice whether there are new messages. Subscribing doesn't cost you anything and is the most convenient option of you are going to be a frequent reader of a particular newsgroup.

Subscribing is easy. If you use Microsoft Internet News, simply click the **Subscribe** button after selecting the newsgroup in the newsgroup window. If you use Netscape Navigator News Reader, click the checkbox next to the news group name in the **News Server** window.

Posting and Responding to Messages

It's always a good idea to follow a newsgroup for a while before posting messages yourself. Reading messages and never posting is called *lurking*. Lurk for a few days so you will know what type of messages and topics are appropriate for the list.

Replies to messages can be posted to the newsgroup for all participants to see, or you can send a personal reply to the message author by E-mail.

You can also start a new thread by posting your own message to the newsgroup. This is very similar to sending E-mail, but instead of addressing the message to one person you post it to the list for all participants to see.

Responsible Participation: Newsgroup Etiquette

All the etiquette rules that apply to E-mail apply to newsgroups as well. Since messages in newsgroups may be read by thousands of people, however, there are a few additional rules you should keep in mind.

Keep it short. Keep your messages to newsgroups short and to the point. Many people have to pay for access to the Internet and the extra time needed to download long or off-topic messages costs them money.

Don't believe everything you read. There's no control over what's posted in most newsgroups, so you're likely to find all types of information. Some of it is profane and inflammatory, and some of it is just plain wrong. If you are easily offended you should be careful which newsgroups you read. Be careful about believing anything you read in a newsgroup, especially if it's some type of rumor or gossip. Some people make a sport out of posting outlandish rumors, or intentionally post factually incorrect information. When you read a message in a newsgroup, pay attention to the name of the author. Pretty soon you will figure out who is reliable and who isn't. Newsgroups are a great source of information and peer support, but don't believe everything you read. If you have children, you may want to restrict their access to newsgroups. Many contain language and content that's not appropriate for children.

Be tolerant. Newsgroups are read by people all over the world, many of whom do not use English as their native language. Never flame or correct anyone's spelling or grammar, and be very tolerant of misused phrases or "broken English."

Don't send spam. Easy access to the Internet has spawned a new breed of junk mail known as *spam*. Spam is a message promising a new way to loose weight, get rich quick, or something similar. Some of these messages are chain letters, others are outright scams and hoaxes. A spam message is never about the topic of the newsgroup to which it has been posted. Don't respond to spam messages, and do not post off-topic messages like that yourself!

Keep cross posting to a minimum. *Cross posting* means that a message will be sent to more than one newsgroup simultaneously. This can be compared to running from room to room at a party and carrying on the same conversation with different groups of people. Since many people who read newsgroups follow many groups on similar topics, cross posted messages almost always reach the same audience anyway. It is very annoying to see similar, but slightly different threads in different newsgroups. Never post a message to more than two or three newsgroups, and be sure you have a very good reason for doing so.

Group Discussion via E-mail (Listservers)

part

1

Setting up a newsgroup is not an easy process, so many special interest groups use a variation of E-mail to pass messages to all of the group members. A *listserver* is a program that automatically distributes messages to all the members of the list. Once you join a list, the listserver will send you all messages via standard E-mail. You can reply to a message or start a new discussion by sending an E-mail message to the listserver program instead of sending copies of a message to each member individually.

Listservers are convenient because they insure that all members of the list see all the posted messages, including all replies between members. Some listserver programs will accumulate and combine messages into a *digest*. A digest allows the listserver to send one large message to each member on a periodic basis rather than sending many small messages all the time. For very active lists it's easier for the members and more efficient for the Internet for list members to use the digest form.

Finding a Mailing List

There are thousands of mailing lists, so how do you find lists on your favorite topics? There are several ways. First, you will see references to lists as you read newsgroups and carry on discussions with colleagues.

Second, there are some resources on the World Wide Web that you can search by topic to find the names of mailing lists that may be of interest. And third, you can obtain lists of lists via E-mail.

ERIC can be a good source of education-related electronic discussion groups. For example, ERIC/EECE currently sponsors eight lists for people interested in issues related to Elementary and Early Childhood Education. These groups operate on Listserv software on the University of Illinois' "postoffice" computer: http://ericps.crc.uiuc.edu/eece/listserv.html.

■ **CAMPUSCARE-L**

This list addresses the concerns of the staff, faculty, and administrators in laboratory schools or children's centers on university or college campuses, in early childhood education departments, and in family-work programs.

■ **ECENET-L**

This discussion group is a forum for the consideration of issues related to the development, education, and care of children from birth through age 8. It is intended for teacher educators, researchers, policymakers, teachers, students, and parents. An archive of messages posted to ECENET-L is located on the Gopher of the ERIC Clearinghouse on Information & Technology at Syracuse University.

■ **ECPOLICY-L**

ECPOLICY-L is co-sponsored by the National Association for the Education of Young Children and ERIC/EECE. Discussion centers on policy issues pertaining to children and families, child care, preschool education, and related concerns. An archive of messages posted to ECPOLICY-L is located on the Gopher of the ERIC Clearinghouse on Information & Technology at Syracuse University.

■ **ECPROFDEV-L**

ECPROFDEV-L will foster communication among those who teach pre-service and in-service early childhood educators, train Head Start or other early childhood program staff, and consult or facilitate learning with early childhood professionals in any setting. Among other topics, discussion will center on the varying philosophies in approaching the education and training of diverse groups in early childhood education, the design of learning activities, and new resources, assessment, and other issues related to fostering learning. An archive of messages posted to ECPROFDEV-L is located on the

part

1

Gopher of the ERIC Clearinghouse on Information & Technology at Syracuse University.

■ **MIDDLE-L**

MIDDLE-L provides a place for sharing ideas, information about resources, and problems and their solutions related to middle level education. It is intended for middle level educators, teacher educators, and others interested in education at the middle level. An archive of messages posted to MIDDLE-L is located on the Gopher of the ERIC Clearinghouse on Information & Technology at Syracuse University.

■ **PARENTING-L**

PARENTING-L is a discussion group for parents who want to share their concerns and questions about family life in the 1990s, including child-raising and parent involvement in children's education. An archive of messages posted to PARENTING-L is located on the Gopher of the ERIC Clearinghouse on Information & Technology at Syracuse University.

■ **PROJECTS-L**

This discussion group focuses on the Project Approach, which is "an in-depth study of a topic undertaken by a class, a group, or an individual child," as the approach is used in early childhood, elementary, and middle level classrooms. The list, co-owned by Sylvia Chard at the University of Alberta and by ERIC/EECE, will be operational around the end of February, 1996.

■ **REGGIO-L**

Early childhood programs in Reggio Emilia, Italy, are internationally acclaimed. This discussion group, co-sponsored by ERIC/EECE and the Merrill Palmer Institute at Wayne State Univ., provides a forum for discussing the Reggio Emilia approach to early education. An archive of messages posted to REGGIO-L is located on the Gopher of the ERIC Clearinghouse on Information & Technology at Syracuse University.

■ **SAC-L**

SAC-L is a discussion group for those interested in school-age care planning, resources, funding, and related topics. SAC-L is co-owned by the School-Age Child Care Project at the Center for Research on Women (Wellesley College) & ERIC/EECE. An archive of messages posted to SAC-L is located on the Gopher of the ERIC Clearinghouse on Information & Technology at Syracuse University.

part
1

Participating in Discussions

To participate in a mailing list discussion you must subscribe to or join the list. Each list has two addresses, the sub scription or listserver address, and the submissions address. Use the listserver address to join or quit the list; use the submissions address to send a message to members of the mailing list. Listserver addresses almost always start with "listserv," "listproc," or "majordomo."

Specific instructions for subscribing depend on how the list was set up, but the normal procedure to subscribe to a list is:

1. Send an E-mail message to the listserver by putting the listserver's address on the "To:" line of the message. Do not use the submission address for the list!

2. Leave the subject line of the message blank. If your E-mail program will not let you send a message with a blank subject, use "subscribe" on the subject line.

3. If the name of the listserver has "listserv" or "listserve" in it, type "subscribe *listname*" as the body of the message (where you will substitute the name of the list for *listname*). If the listserver name has the word "mailbase" in it, use the same procedure substituting the word "join" for "subscribe."

In a short time you will receive E-mail telling you that your subscription request has been accepted, or you will get back an error message saying that the listserver did not understand your subscription request. If you get an error message the best thing to do is to send a one-line message to the listserver address that simply says "help." This will usually get you an E-mail message with all the details on how to subscribe to a list on that listserver.

Save the notice the listserver sends when you are finally enrolled as a subscriber. This notice will contain useful information such as how to get off the list, whether or not a digest form is available and how to receive it, how to get back issues, and so on.

After your subscription has been accepted the listserver will start forwarding to you, via E-mail, all messages submitted to the list. You can participate in the discussion by sending an E-mail message to the submission address. Remember that your message will be forwarded to many people, so follow the rules of netiquette.

part

1

If you subscribe to an active list, be sure to read your E-mail frequently. Some lists generate hundreds of messages a week, and your mailbox will fill up quickly if you don't log on frequently to clean it up. You may want to investigate the use of "mail filtering rules" or "inbox assistant" features of your mail reader program to automatically sort messages into folders as they arrive in your mailbox. Check the **Help** section of your mail program for the details of using these features.

The Internet as a Library: Using the Web for Research

The fastest and most popular part of the Internet is the World Wide Web. The Web consists of hundreds of thousands of computers, each publishing information you can use. Some of the information is very useful, such as on-line library card catalogs, information from organizations, and subject-specific information you can't find anywhere else. You'll also find loads of useless, tasteless, and incorrect information and propaganda. On the Web, everyone and anyone can be a publisher.

part

1

The web got its name because each site usually contains *links* to other sites the publisher thinks are related. Since each site has links to other sites, a kind of web is formed. This is the great power of the Web. Once you find a site that contains information you find useful, you can follow the links to other sites you think may be interesting then continue with your research. This is like using the bibliography of one book to find other books, only much faster.

Structure of the Web: Making Order out of Chaos

Unfortunately, there's no overall organization for Web sites—no classification system or central catalog. Anyone can publish information on the Web. The result can be compared to a library without a book numbering system or card catalog. You must roam around until you happen to find what you are looking for.

The trick to finding information on the Web is to keep a short list of sites that specialize in cataloging information from other Web sites, keep your own personal list of favorite Web sites, and learn to use at least one of the many *search engines* that will scan the Internet looking for Web sites that contain keywords or phrases that you specify.

Navigating the Web

Navigating the Web requires a program called a *browser*. The browser keeps track of where you are on the Web and displays the information sent to your computer by the Web site. Using the Web is an interactive process. Information is sent to you as you request it.

Information on the Web is independent of the type of computer you are using. It doesn't matter if you are using a Macintosh or PC-compatible. To view information on any site, all you need is a browser for your specific computer.

There are several browsers on the market, but the two most popular are Netscape Navigator and Microsoft Internet Explorer. We'll show examples from both of those browsers in this section.

part

1

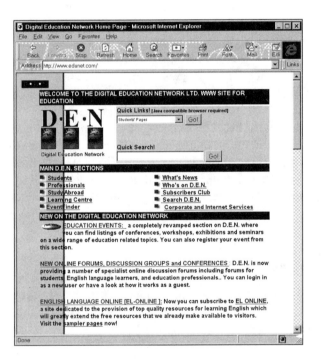

All browsers offer similar basic functions. The basic functions are:

- Site Name Selection: Go to a specific Web site
- HyperText Link: Move to a new site when an on-screen link is selected
- **Back** button: Back up to the previous site
- **Forward** button: Move forward to return to the site you just moved back from

- **Home** button: Go to your home or starting page
- **Print** button: Print the current page
- **Refresh** button: Refresh the current display

Uniform Resource Locators (URLs) Each site on the Web has an address called a Uniform Resource Locator, or *URL*. The URL always starts with the letters "http://". The colon and two slash characters are required. These letters tell the Web browser that the address you are about to give is for a Web site. Next comes the name of the site itself. Most, but not all, Web sites use the letters "www" as the first part of their name. For example, Microsoft's Web site's address is "http://www.microsoft.com" and the Web site for the University of Illinois in Urbana-Champaign is at "http://www.uiuc.edu".

You can often guess the Web site address for large companies by typing "http://www. *name*.com", putting the company name or abbreviation in place of *name*. For example, Allyn and Bacon's Web site address is "http://www.abacon.com". Many other sites have obvious names as well. *College Net* has a Web site at "http://www.college.com". It is a place to find information about music, art, organizations, and publications of interest to students or by students.

part

1

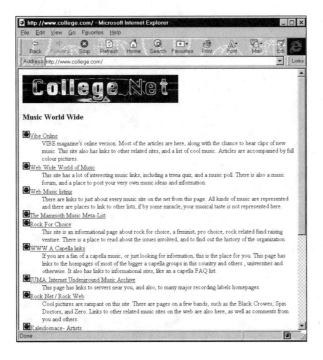

The toolbar at the top of your browser window contains a place for you to type the address of the Web site you want to see. In Netscape Navigator it's labeled "Go to:" and in Microsoft Internet Explorer it's labeled "Address:". Both programs expect you to type the URL in exactly the same format. The URL for the site and page you are currently viewing will be displayed in this area as you navigate your way around the Web.

When you start your browser it will always take you to the same starting point or *home page*. The home page will usually contain links to other sites and so enables you to begin your Web exploration from a known point.

Browser Basics The actual display of information from a Web site depends on the computer you have, the browser you are using, and the features programmed into the Web page by the publisher. Some pages are only text; others are complex multimedia affairs that incorporate sound and video. Your browser will do its best to display the information from a site on your computer even if you do not have all the options required. For example, if your computer does not have sound capability, the browser will not try to play audio tracks from Web sites that incorporate them.

part

1

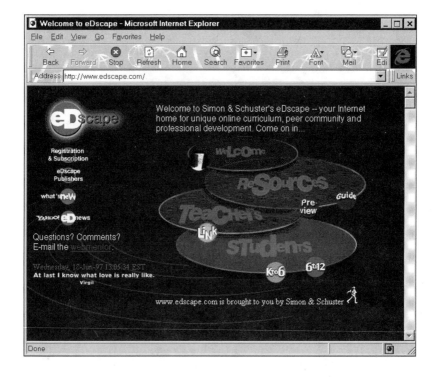

HyperText When you look at a page in the browser window you'll see some highlighted words and phrases. The highlight is usually a different color than the main text as well as an underline. Highlighted phrases are the *links* to other pages on the Web. Click your mouse on a highlighted phrase and the browser will jump you to the appropriate location. This type of text with embedded links to related details is called *hypertext.*

part

1

Some links are to programs or data files that can be downloaded to your computer. When you click on one of these links you will see a box asking for permission to download the file. Choose the "Save File" button on the dialog and the file will be sent to your computer.

Image Maps As the design of Web pages became more sophisticated, it was soon discovered that text links were inconvenient for many applications. For example, a site with weather information on the continental US would be easier to navigate if the user clicked a point on a map instead of choosing a location from a long list of text links. With this simple idea the *image map* was born.

Many sites incorporate image maps for quick navigation. You will see many uses of image maps as you navigate the Web. As you move your mouse cursor over a graphic, the pointer will change to indicate that the graphic is a clickable image map.

part

1

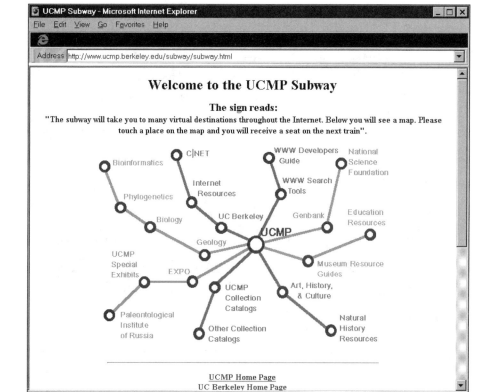

Using Bookmarks and History Files All browsers allow you to set electronic bookmarks, which enable you to return to a Web page without going through other links. This is useful when you find a site you think would be interesting to explore when you have more time, or when you finally find what you're looking for after following dozens of links.

Netscape Navigator files bookmarks under the **Bookmark** menu and Microsoft Internet Explorer files them in the **Favorites** menu, but they work the same way. When you reach a site you want to bookmark:

1. Select the **Add Bookmark** option from the **Bookmark** menu in Navigator, or the **Add to Favorites** option from the **Favorites** menu in Internet Explorer.

2. Navigator immediately adds the site name to the **Bookmark** menu. Internet Explorer pops up a window that allows you to edit the name of the site and to organize your bookmarked favorites in folders.

To return to a bookmarked site, pull down the **Bookmark** menu in Navigator or the **Favorites** menu in Internet Explorer and click on the name of the bookmark.

Your browser is also recording the name of every Web site you visit as you surf around the net. This is called a *history file* and lets you return to any site you have visited recently. Netscape Navigator gives you access to the history file from the **History** option in the **Window** menu. Microsoft Internet Explorer shows the history file via the **Open History Folder** option in the **Go** menu.

part

1

Customizing the Browser

You will find browsing the Web more convenient if you modify the browser to suite your personal taste and needs. The most common customizations are:

- Choosing fonts and colors
- Turning graphics, audio, and video on and off for faster browsing
- Choosing a start page

Netscape Navigator To customize Netscape Navigator, select **General Preferences** from the **Options** menu. The sections available include Appearance, Fonts, Colors, Images, Apps, Helpers, and Language.

Appearance

The Appearance page allows you to make modifications by using fonts, colors, and images.

Toolbars Changes the way the toolbar in the main Netscape Navigator window is displayed. If you have a small monitor you may want to select "Text" style to reduce the space taken by the Toolbar.

Startup Specifies whether Netscape Navigator will show the Web browser, mail reader, or news reader when it first starts. You can also specify a Web page to act as a jumping-off point every time you start the browser. This is useful if you always want to begin with a search engine or the Web page from a specific organization.

Link Styles These options affect the way links are displayed and how long history files are kept. Leave these options at their default settings until you get more experience with Netscape Navigator. Then you can check the Help section for more detailed information on their use.

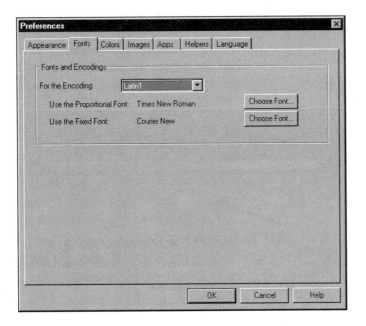

Fonts

The Fonts page lets you change the basic font Netscape Navigator uses to display the text on Web pages. There are two fonts you can set. The proportional font is used for all "normal" text. You may want to decrease the size of this font so the browser can show more of the page in the window, or you may prefer to increase the size of the font to make the pages easier to read. The fixed font is used for some tabular material, and does not have as great an effect on the readability of the display.

Do not change the *Encoding* selection unless you routinely visit non-English language sites and have a specific reason to make the change.

Colors

The Color settings are the default values used by Netscape Navigator if the Web publisher does not use specific colors. Links is the color of a link on the Web page. Followed Links is for links that point to sites you have seen recently. Text is the standard text color, and Background is the standard page background color. The default values are probably acceptable unless you discern certain colors better than others.

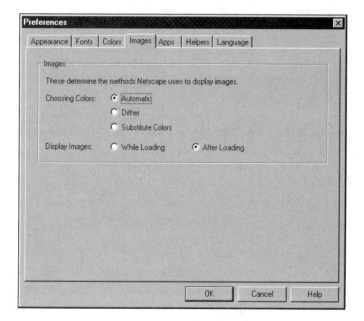

Images

This page lets you specify how Netscape Navigator will handle pictures displayed on Web pages. Leave the Color setting set to Automatic. If you have a modem on your computer and connect to the Web over a telephone line, you may find Web browsing faster if you change the Display Images selection to "After loading." This tells Netscape Navigator to load and display all text on the page, then the pictures. This setting can save you time. After reading some or all of the text while the graphics load, you may decide the site is not useful and go on to another without waiting for the pictures. Try the setting both ways to see which you like best.

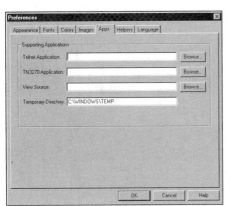

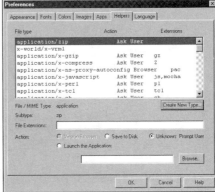

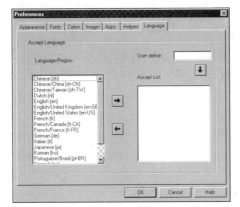

part

1

Apps, Helpers, and Language

Do not make any changes to the settings on the Apps, Helpers, or Language pages unless you have very specific reasons for doing so, and have the assistance of an experienced user.

Microsoft Internet Explorer To customize the Microsoft Internet Explorer, select **Options** from the **View** menu. The option categories are listed on the "tabs" near the top of the screen: General, Connection, Navigation, Programs, Security, and Advanced.

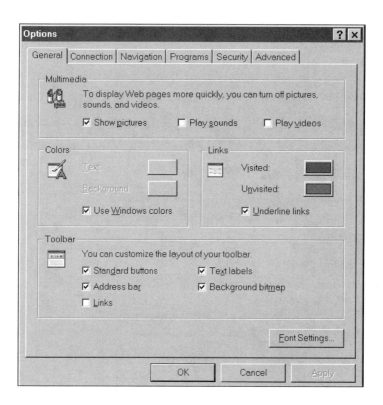

General

The General options control the overall look of the browser.

Multimedia   Some Web pages include graphics, sound, and video: the Multimedia section controls which special effects Internet Explorer will download from the page. If you are connected to the Internet using a modem and telephone line, you can speed up the display of Web pages by turning off all three options. This is useful when you're surfing the Web and want to quickly scan pages. You won't have to wait for the multimedia effects to download to your computer; you will be able to move through pages much faster. When you find the page you're looking for, turn on the options you want.

Color, Links The Colors and Links controls allow you to customize the appearance of Web pages. These should normally be left at their default values.

Toolbar The Toolbar control lets you change the appearance and size of the toolbar. This is useful when you become an expert user and want to reduce the amount of screen space used by the toolbar.

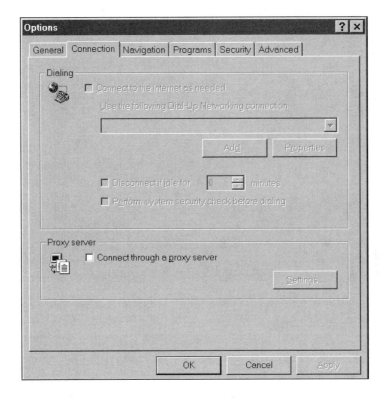

part

1

Connection

Do not change the options on the Connection page unless you have specific instructions to do so. These options are set by the installer of the browser. If you make any changes here incorrectly, the browser will not work.

Navigation

The Navigation page allows you to change the Start page, Search page and links Toolbar page. You can also set the number of pages to record in the history file.

Customize The Navigation page lets you change the browser's "Start Page," the page that automatically displays each time the browser starts. This is useful if you always want to begin with a search engine or the Web page from a specific organization. You can also change this entry to the file "C:\WINDOWS\SYSTEM\BLANK.HTM" which is an empty page. This setting makes the browser start faster and is useful when you do not stay on the same page each time you start the browser.

History The History section controls the amount of space the browser will use to maintain your Web page viewing history. These options are normally left at their default values unless you are given specific instructions to change them.

Programs, Advanced, and Security Pages

Do not make changes to the settings on these pages unless you are given specific instructions.

Searching for Information

When you start on a research project it's sometimes hard to know where to look for information. With so many diverse sites on the Web it would be impossible to visit them yourself looking for information. A whole new breed of programs called *search engines* will do the looking for you. A search engine looks through a giant index of Web pages which is created by robot programs that roam the Web collecting and indexing information. The index on the largest of the search sites, AltaVista (http://altavista.digital.com), contains information from 31 million pages on 476,000 Web sites. The search engine will look through this massive index for key words and phrases in a fraction of a second! AltaVista displays a link for any page that contains the words you specify anywhere on the page.

Another popular search engine is maintained by *Yahoo!* (http:// www.yahoo.com), a company that maintains an index of Web sites. The *Yahoo!* search engine is based on categories and shows links to Web sites that cover topics you specify.

Using a Search Engine AltaVista indexes the contents of Web sites, *Yahoo!* organizes Web sites into categories. The difference in approach gives vastly different search results. *Yahoo!* returned a list of 5564 categories that had the word "literacy" somewhere in their title or category name. AltaVista, on the other hand, found more than 200,000 pages of information that use the word "literacy."

You should choose an index like *Yahoo!* when you are looking for sites that cover a specific category of information, like "Literacy." Use AltaVista when there is something very specific you are looking for, like "childhood literacy."

part

1

1. Simple Searches Start your browser and go to URL http://altavista. digital.com. (You should also set a bookmark for AltaVista so you can come back here without remembering this URL.)

2. Type "childhood literacy" in the search box and click the **Submit** button. AltaVista will search its index for all Web pages that have the words "childhood" and "literacy". The results of your search will be returned to you in a few seconds.

3. You'll see that "childhood" was found more than 206,000 times and "literacy" was also found more than 206,000 times. Clearly this search is not usable.

4. Now type "childhood+literacy" as the search string and click **Submit**. The '+' sign is very important. It ties the words together; now AltaVista will only find sites that contain the *phrase* "childhood literacy". This time about 55 sites are returned. That's few enough to be of some value.

5. Type "childhood+literacy Graves" and click **Submit**. Because you have entered more words the search actually returns more sites (about 3,000 this time), but this time AltaVista will organize them so the sites with the highest frequency of matching words appear first on the list. Chances are that if you were doing research on Graves you would find what you are looking for within the first few pages of links.

The moral here is to be as specific as possible when using a massive index search engine and try to trim down the number of sites returned. You will also notice that the search engines try to sort the sites they find based on the relevance of the words you specify. Each search engine uses a complicated, proprietary formula to try to bring the sites that are most likely to be of interest to the top of the list. As you scroll down the list the links will be father and farther off-topic, and there's no need to continue looking. You're better off submitting another search with a slightly different set of words and phrases to see if you can find anything else.

Now use the URL "http://www.yahoo.com" to point your browser at *Yahoo!*. Type "childhood literacy" in the search box and click the **Search** option. *Yahoo!*'s classification scheme finds 1260 sites with "childhood literacy" in the title.

See what a difference the indexing technique makes? *Yahoo!* finds many fewer sites that have relevant information because it's only looking at Web page titles. If an educator has written an article on childhood literacy, *Yahoo!* won't find the page, but AltaVista will.

Try searches in both sites and see which you like best. You can also try these other search engines, one of which may be more to your liking:

Excite	http://www.excite.com
Info Seek	http://www.infoseek.com
Lycos	http://www.lycos.com
Web Crawler	http://www.webcrawler.com

part

1

Avoiding Information Overload: Advanced Search Techniques

Some of the search engines offer an *advanced* or *custom* search mode which enables you to use special commands to narrow or widen a search. The most common special commands are:

AND

Use AND to narrow a search. This command causes the search engine to find Web pages that include all of the keywords you specify. For example, the search

Piaget AND Vygotsky

will find Web pages that use both names. A page that uses only one of these names will not be found by the search. The AND command is a great tool when you know exactly what you're looking for.

NEAR

The NEAR command is used to find any Web pages on which two words are "close" to each other. For example:

Skinner NEAR Reinforcement

will find Web pages that include phrases such as "Skinner studied reinforcement," and "Jim Skinner provided reinforcement." Different search engines have different tolerances for "closeness," but the words you specify must usually be between six or eight words of each other to be found by a NEAR search.

OR

OR is used to widen a search when you're not sure how to find what you want. This command will locate all Web pages that include any of the keywords you specify. For example,

holistic scoring OR rubric

will find any Web page that mentions either or both of these terms. The OR command greatly increases the number of links returned by a search, so it's most often useful when you are starting a research project and want get an idea of what's available.

NOT

Careful use of NOT can narrow a search when you already know that certain keywords should be eliminated. A search like

Reinforcement NOT Positive

will find any Web page with the word "Reinforcement" on it as long as the word "Positive" is not on the same page.

These commands can also be combined. If you are going use the Web for research, it's a good investment of time to learn about these advanced search commands. Click the *Help* link in the search engine you like best to read about the various advanced searching features it offers.

Security on the Web

Avoiding Scam Artists and Credit Card Fraud Mail order catalog shopping has taken on new heights with on-line shopping via the Web. There

part

1

are many on-line "storefronts" offering all types of merchandise and services for sale. Most of these operations are legitimate, but there are a few fly-by-night operators setting up Web sites. Use the same cautions you would use when shopping by mail or telephone.

- Know who you're dealing with. Be careful when dealing with companies or people you have never heard of.
- If a deal sounds too good to be true, it probably is.
- Be sure the company offers a money-back guarantee so you can return merchandise that you don't like.

There's a lot of publicity about credit card fraud on the Web, but it's not really much different than giving your credit card to a waiter in a restaurant. Someone at a store can write down your card number just as easily as the number can be recorded over the Web. The main rule is to know who you are dealing with and use some common sense. Be sure to check your credit card statements carefully if you start purchasing items over the Web.

part

1

Site Ratings Recent publicity and possible congressional action regarding the availability of pornographic and other explicit materials on the Web have resulted in a Web site rating system developed by the Recreational Software Advisory Council and enforced by the Microsoft Internet Explorer, version 3 and higher. This system, however, is totally voluntary on the part of the Web site operators, so it's by no means a foolproof system. If you want to restrict access to Web sites you find unacceptable or offensive, you should investigate the site rating system features of Internet Explorer by selecting **Options** from the **View** menu and then choosing the **Security** tag.

Virus Protection The Web offers many opportunities for you to download programs and files to your computer. Most of these programs are perfectly safe to download, but be careful when downloading programs from unknown sources. You may be ex posing your computer to a harmful virus. Be especially careful if you download games or recreational programs. If you do a lot of downloading it's worth investing in virus protection software for your computer. A virus scanner looks at programs that you have downloaded and warns you if they contain viruses before the virus has a chance to infect and damage your computer's files.

Sharing Files with Others: FTP

FTP stands for File Transfer Protocol and is the means by which you copy files from someone's computer to yours over the Internet. There are many ways of transferring files, but the easiest one is to use your Web browser.

Both Netscape Navigator and Microsoft Internet Explorer utilize FTP in two ways. The first is by downloading a file when you click a link on a Web page. Links can be set up not only to take you from one page to another, but also to start a file transfer. The second way is to use the browser to browse to an FTP site instead of a Web site.

Retrieving Files from Web Pages

When you are looking at a Web page it's not possible to distinguish browsing links from file links, except by context. Click on an FTP link to activate it. The browser will display a message box asking if you would like to save the file on your computer's disk drive, or open the file.

part

1

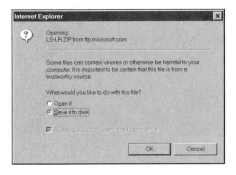

You normally choose to save the file. (If you choose to open the file instead, it will not be saved on your computer.) Choose the *Save* option and confirm the file name. After you confirm the file name a status indicator will appear on the screen.

Retrieving Files from FTP Sites

The URL for a Web site always starts with the letters "http://". For an FTP site the URL always starts with "ftp://". We're going to use Allyn & Bacon's FTP site as an example. The FTP address for Allyn & Bacon is "ftp://ftp.abacon.com". Type this address in your browser's **Go To:** or **Address:** window and press the Enter key. The contents of the FTP site will appear in the browser window.

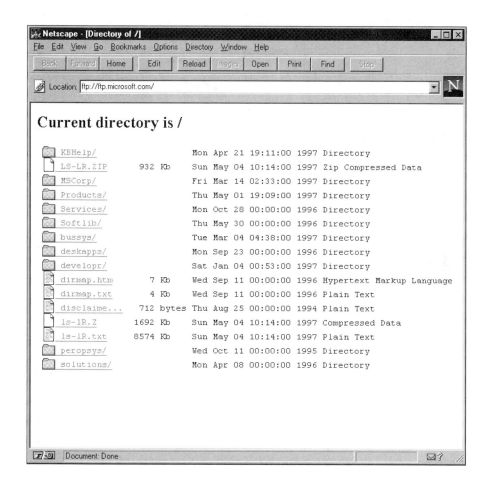

part

1

Netscape Navigator   Netscape Navigator shows the structure of the FTP site by indicating files with an icon that looks like a sheet of paper with a bent corner and directories with an icon that looks like a folder.

To download a file or see what's in a directory, click the highlighted link beside the icon. You will be asked if you want to save or open the file. Choose the *Save* option and the file will be sent to your computer.

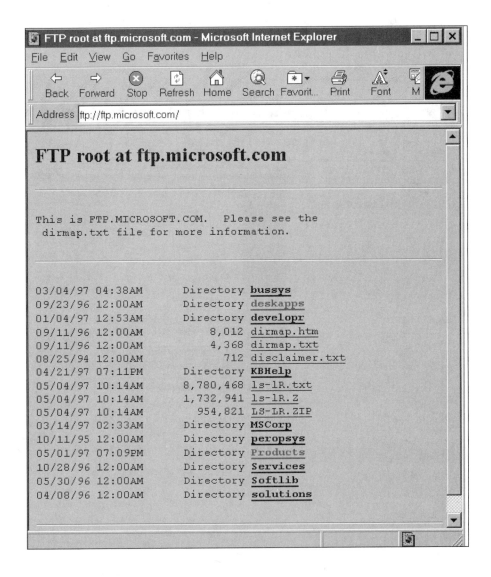

Microsoft Internet Explorer Microsoft Internet Explorer shows the structure of the FTP site by putting the size next to files and the word "DIRECTORY" next to directories. To download a file or see what's in a directory click the highlighted link. Choose the *Save* option when prompted, then confirm the file name and start the download.

The status indicator will show the progress of the download. If you are connecting to the Internet using a phone line and modem, a download may take a long time—possibly hours, especially if the file is more than a few hundred thousand bytes long. Be sure you don't need the phone for while!

Posting Files You can make files available to other people by placing them on an FTP site. Each site has its own procedure for making files available, so you'll have to ask your Internet Service Provider how you can "upload" files to an FTP site so they will be available for other people.

part

1

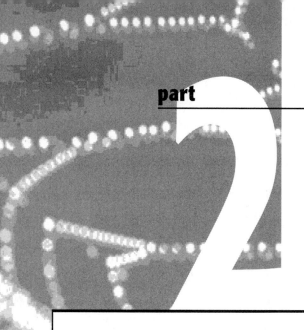

part

Education on the Internet

The following sites are provided for your browsing pleasure. They are arranged alphabetically.

`http://tavi.acomp.usf.edu/foxbox/`

Adam's Fox Box
Fox poems, stories, and information

`http://www.abacon.com`

Allyn and Bacon
Education resources

`gopher://mercury.cair.du.edu:70/11/gophers/`
`public_policy/`

American Association of Core Curriculum
Curriculum resources

`http://www.arc.tulane.edu/`

Amistad Research Center
African-American history & culture

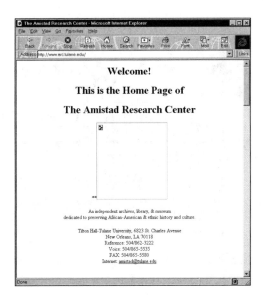

http://artsedge.kennedy-center.org/artsedge.html

ArtsEdge
K–12 art resources

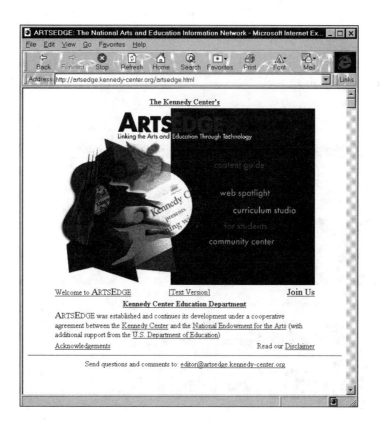

http://ericir.syr.edu

AskERIC Virtual Library
Lesson plans, ERIC digests, tools

http://www.audubon.org/audubon/

Audubon
Birds

part

2

http://www.cs.cmu.edu:8001/Web/People/spok/banned-books.html

Banned Books On-line
Censorship issues

http://www2.portage.net/~dmiddlet/bears/index.html

Bear Den
Bear information

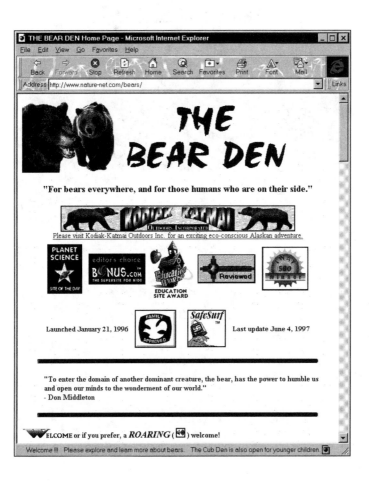

part

2

`http://galaxy.einet.net/galaxy/Science/Biology.html`

Biology
K–12 Science

`http://i-site.on.ca/Isite/Education/Bk_report/`

Book Nook
Book reports by children

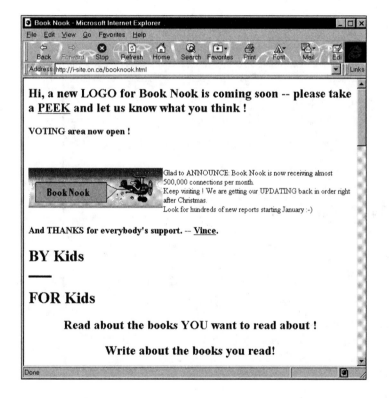

`http://hiddencharms.com/inscape/thyme_in.html`

Bunny Thymes
Animal-related newsletter for children & adults

```
http://www.gatech.edu/1cc/idt/Students/Cole/proj/
K-12/TOC.html
```

Busy Teachers Web Site
K–12 Internet resources

```
http://www.onramp.ca/~lowens/107kids.htm
```

Canadian Kids' Page
Kid stuff

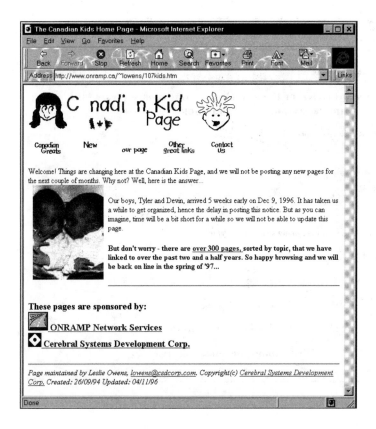

part

2

```
http://www.cweb.com/
```

Career WEB
Career information

`http:www.rpi.edu/dept/cdc/homepage.html`

Career Resources
Career information

`http://http2.sils.umich.edu/~dtorres/cats/cats.html`

Cats on the Internet
Cat photos and information resources

`http://www.wentworth.com/classroom`

Classroom Connect
Online magazine

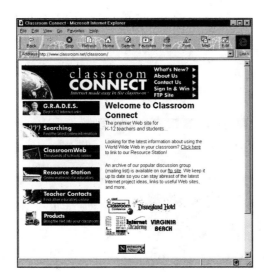

```
http://www.okc.com/fish
```

Cold Spring Fish Hatchery
Hands on indoor outdoor display materials

```
http://www.tpoint.net/~jewels/college.html
```

College Prep Page
Helps students prepare for college

```
http://info.med.yale.edu/comer
```

Comer School Development Program
National school reform project

```
http://www.tc.cornell.edu:80/Edu/MathSciGateway/
```

Cornell Math & Science Gateway
9–12 Math and science resources

part

2

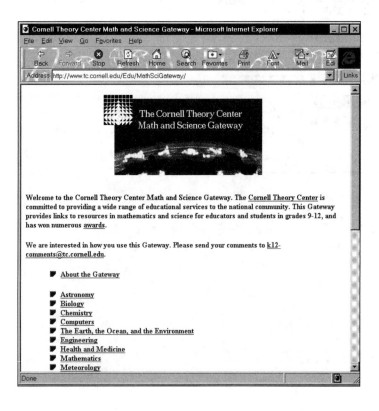

http://www.ascri.fsu.edu/~dennisl/CMS.html

Cyberspace Middle School
Links to on-line middle school resources

http://www.crl.com/~gorgon/distance.html

Distance Learning Resources
List of links and descriptions

http://www.dog-play.com/

Dog-Play
Animal-assisted therapy

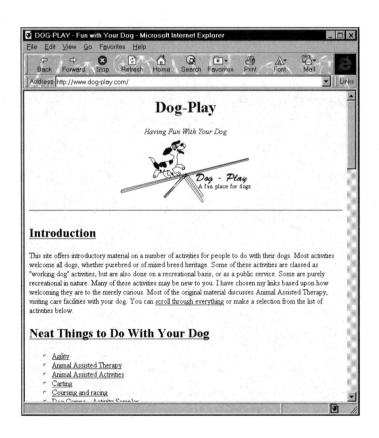

part

2

http://pasture.ecn.purdue.edu/~laird/Dogs/
glossary.html

Dog Term Glossary
Vocabulary

http://mingus.loni.ucla.edu:1028/FURMANSKI/
dolphin2.html

Dolphin Page
Information on the dolphin

http://www.fn.net/education.html

Education Sites
Internet resources

`http://buckman.pps.k12.or.us/election/election.html`

election.html
Depicts voting in "Toon Town"

`http://www.stolaf.edu/network/iecc/`

e-mail Classroom Connections
Key pals for cross-cultural exchange

`http://www.nceet.snreumich.edu/EndSpp/Endangered.html`

Endangered Species
Information and lists

`http://www.exploratorium.edu/`

Exploratorium
Science resources for students, parents, teachers

`http://dca.net:80/exoticpets/`

Exotic Pets
On-line exotic pet shop

part 2

`http://csc.peachnet.edu/~rpoore/Ferrets/`

Ferret World
Pets

`http://www.fred.net/cindy/frednet.html`

FredNet Moo
Virtual educational applications

http://www-hpcc.astro.washington.edu/scied/
galileo.html

Galileo
K–12 Science

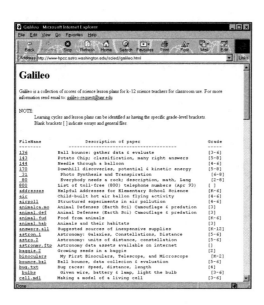

`http://www.tezcat.com/~ermiller/getapet.html`

Getting a Pet
Pet information

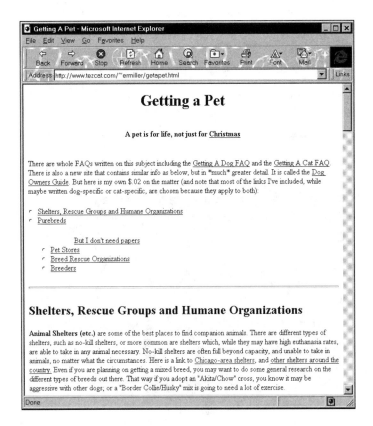

part
2

`http://www.for.nau.edu/~alew/ustxtwlc.html`

Geography USA
Geography resources

`http://forum.swarthmore.edu/`

Geometry Forum
Geometry resources

```
http://lcweb.loc.gov/
```

Government Resources
Assorted links to government

```
http://www.grolier.com
```

Grolier Interactive
On-line encylopedia

```
http://www.helloindia.com
```

Hello, India
Indian food, culture, music

part

2

http://www.carto.com

Heritage Map Museum
15th–19th Century maps

http://www.eskimo.com/~billb/home.html

Home Schooling
Assorted resources

http://www.tpoint.net/~jewels/homework.html

Homework Page
Resources by subject

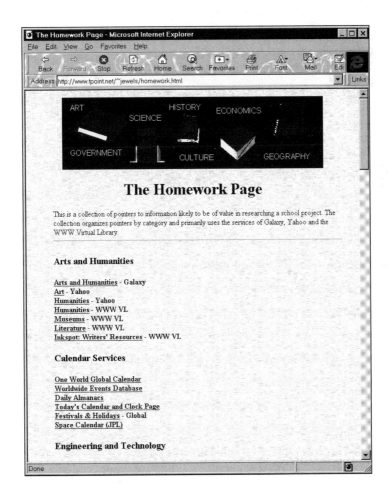

http://www.thinktek.com/horses.htm

Horse Zone
Animal information

http://www.igc.apc.org/iearn/

I*Earn
International links

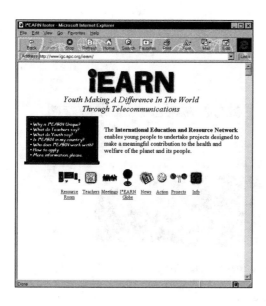

part

2

http://www.sln.fi.edu/qanda3.html

Inquiry Almanac
Science education

http://www.interlog.com/~ohi/inkspots/young.html

Inkspot
Young writers

http://curry.edschool.Virginia.edu:80/~insttech/frog/

Interactive Frog Dissection
Science

http://www.aber.ac.uk/~magwww/index_ht1.html

Internet Educational resources
Education links, on-line magazines, tools

http://www.umassd.edu/SpecialPrograms/ISN/
Kidnews.html

ISN Kidnews
News service for students

http://seawifs.gsfc.nasa.gov/scripts/JASON.html

JASON
World wide collaborative learning projects

http://www.interport.net/~sachi

Kid's Space
Enhancing baic computer skills

http://pathfinder.com/@@egQ6VwAAAAAAIMR/Life/lifehome.html

Life Magazine
Current events photos

http://www.frontiertech.com/gall.htm

Lion Gallery
Lion stories, poems, facts, information

part

2

http://the-tech.mit.edu/Shakespeare/works.html.

Literature
Shakespeare

http://quest.arc.nasa.gov/livefrom/livefrom.html

Live from Antarctica
Field journals, resources

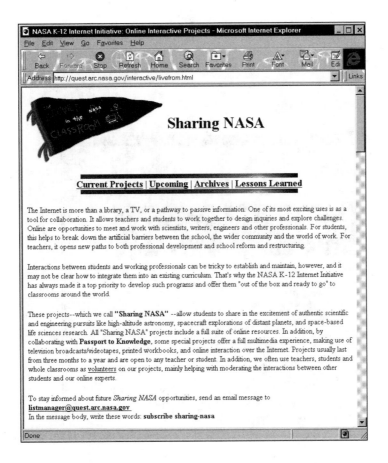

part

2

http://hydor.colorado.edu/twain/

Mark Twain Library
Electronic text versions

http://www.teleport.com/~vincer/math.html

Math Education Resources
Plans, guides, links

http://forum.swarthmore.edu/mathmagic/

MathMagic
World wide K–12 team problem solving

http://www.nyu.edu/pages/mathmol/

Mathmol
Molecular modeling for K–12

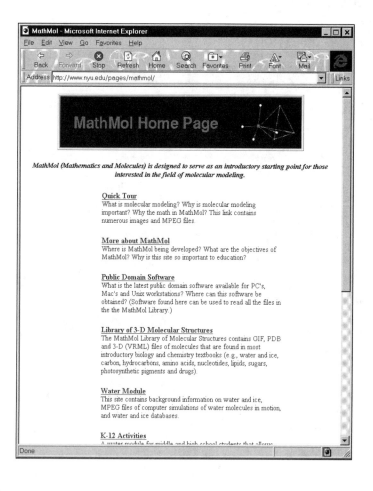

`http://www.c3.lanl.gov/mega-math/welcome.html`

Megamath
Elementary math resources

`http://www.netaxs.com~mhmyers/image.html#birdtel`

Michael's Photo Gallery
Bird photos

`http://volcano.und.nodak.edu/vwdocs/msh/msh.html`

Mt. St. Helens
Images and text on volcano

`http://quest.arc.nasa.gov/OER/`

NASA Education
Science resources

`http://nysernet.org`

NYSERNet
Teaching tools and reference information

`http://www.cs.smu.edu/Web/references.html`

On-line Reference Books
Assorted dictionaries and reference books

**part
2**

http://www.novia.net/~video

Parenting Skills on Video
Parenting skills

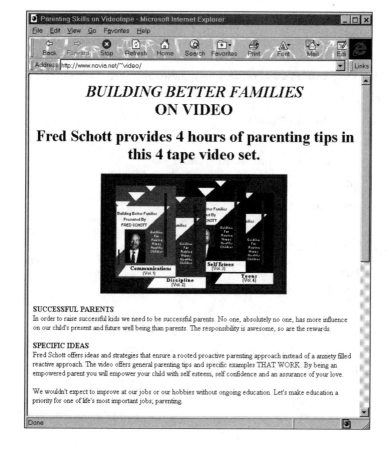

http://turnpike.net/emporium/C/celestial/epsm.htm

Prehistoric Shark Museum
Fossil shark remains

http://www.thinkthink.com/schools/

Private Schools On-line
Private prep school information

http://www.brigadoon.com/psrnet/

Private Schools Resource
Resources for private schools

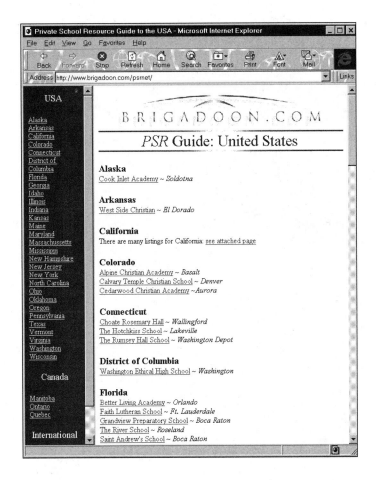

http://osman.classics.washington.edu/libellus/
libellus.html

Project Libellus
Greek and Latin texts

http://www.reedbooks.com.au/index.html

Reed Global Classroom
International key pal search, projects, collaborations

http://www.bev.net/education/SeaWorld/homepage.html

SeaWorld
Animal information

http://www.screen.com/streetcents.html

Street Cents
Youth consumer information

http://www.sentex.net/~casaa

Student Leadership
Leadership materials and ideas

part
2

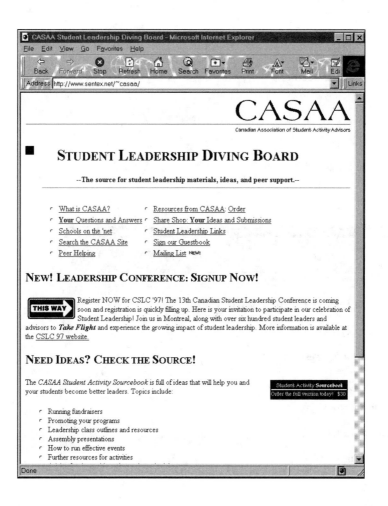

part

2

http://teams.lacoe.edu/

TEAMSnet
Preservice teacher resources

http://www.cochran.com/

Theodore Tugboat
Interactive stories

http://www.demon.co.uk/sharpsw/total.html

Total Recall
Memory enhancement

http://www.ntt.jp/japan/japanese/

Traveler's Japanese
Basic language skills

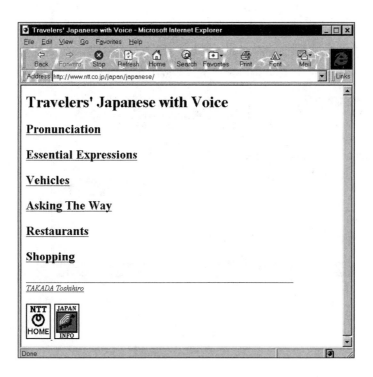

http://eric-web.tc.columbia.edu/

UEWeb
Urban education

http://www.usatoday.com/web1.htm

USA Today
On-line newspaper

```
http://sln.fi.edu/tfi/jump.html
```

Virtual Exhibits
Assorted interactive exhibits

```
http://web66.coled.umn.edu
```

Web 66
Integrating the internet in K–12 settings

```
http://www.cwc.lsu.edu/
```

Welcome to the Civil War
Civil War resources

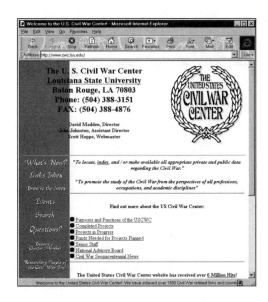

part

2

http://cury.edschool.Virginia.EDU/~kpj5e/Whales/
Contents.HTML

Whales
K–5 thematic units

http://www.macmedia.com.au/whales/

Whale Information Network
Animal resources

http://kingfish.ssp.nmfs.gov/songs.html

Whale Songs
Audio resources

http://www2.whitehouse.gov/WH/Wekcome.html

White House Home Page
Government resources

part
2

http://www.kiae.su/www/wtr/

Window to Russia
On-line art, language, studies

http://sln.fi.edu/franklin/rotten.html

World of Benjamin Franklin
History

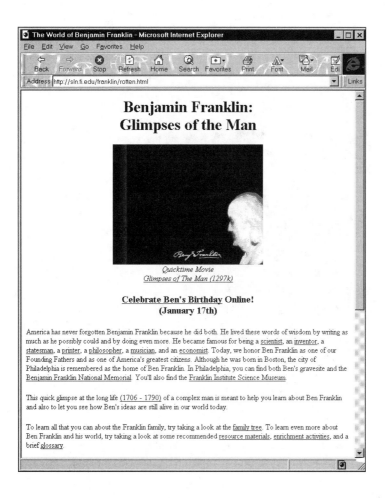

http://www.webpub.com/worldkids/

World Kids
Preschool introduction to foreign language

```
http://www.w3.org/hypertext/DataSources/bySubject/
Overview.html
```

WWW Virtual Library
Maps, country information, cross-referenced themes

```
http://www.missouri.edu/~wleric/writery.html
```

Writing at MU
Discussion site for writers

```
http://sensemedia.net/sprawl/38047
```

Zoo
On-line zoo

part
2

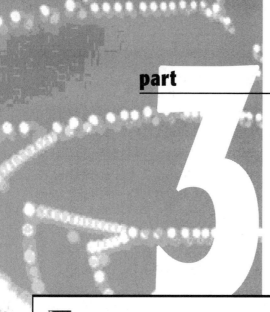

Using the Internet in the Classroom

Lesson Launchers

What follows are just a few ideas to help you begin brainstorming fun and interesting lesson plans. After all, the best plans have to start with ideas! Keep in mind that I do not know the grade you are interested in teaching or for which subject you might want to develop a plan. These lesson launchers are simply notions to help you brainstorm. Noone could ever compile an exhaustive list of the many different ways of using Internet technology in the classroom. Once you begin using the Internet yourself, you'll be able to come up with many more ideas. Undoubtedly you will then think *your* ideas are much better than mine!

Please note: Observe all the appropriate *cautions* discussed in this Quick Guide!

Career day: Gather information from on-line resources. It's amazing to consider the host of professions represented! Possible starting points:
Career WEB—http://www.cweb.com/
Career Resources—http:www.rpi.edu/dept/cdc/homepage.html

College prep: Get ready for those pesky admission exam require-ments, gather information on colleges and universities your Seniors might like to attend, or read campus newspapers. Possible starting points:
College Prep Page—http://www.tpoint.net/~jewels/college.html

Current events: Use any of the conventional newspaper activities that are available, but make the assignment an on-line effort instead of a paper and pen affair. Possible starting points:

USA Today—http://www.usatoday.com/web1.htm

Life Magazine—http://pathfinder.com/@@egQ6VwAAAAAAIMR/
Life/lifehome.html

Environment: The Internet is filled with environmental forums which deal with many of the issues K–12 educators frequently tackle. Add a technological component to your environmental units. Possible starting points: Search AOL with key word "**EForum**", Compuserve with "**Go Earth**", or Prodigy with "**JUMP: Green Connection**". Interesting Internet Gopher sites include "**envirolink.org**", "**greenpeace.org**", or "**gopher.epa.gov**".

Folk tales: AOL features the **American Folktale Project** wherein students can write their own stories for others to read and discuss.

Geography: The Internet is a great place to learn about geography and collect maps from around the world. AOL has some really nice sources, including "ABC", "Library", or "National Geographic". Other starting points:

Geography USA—http://www.for.nau.edu/~alew/ustxtwlc.html

Heritage Map Museum—http://www.carto.com/

Government: E-mail the President or various government officials.

White House Home Page—http://www2.whitehouse.gov/WH/
Wekcome.html

Library of Congress: Access a few of the thousands of treasures from the WWW. Enter: http://lcweb.loc.gov/.

Literature: Do you know William Shakespeare has a Web site? The ideas for a Lit teacher are endless. Enter the following address:

http://the-tech.mit.edu/Shakespeare/works.html.

Pen-Pals: A long-standing favorite can be updated via Internet E-mail. Consider the many other ways to improve the writing process on-line.

I*Earn—http://www.igc.apc.org/iearn/

part

3

Pets: Do science reports on the pets represented in your class. There are a host of newsgroups about pets.

Ferret World—http://csc.peachnet.edu/~rpoore/Ferrets/
Getting a Pet- http://www.tezcat.com/~ermiller/getapet.html

 ## Innovative Internet Applications

Listed below are numerous applications of Internet technology for teachers and students. They include a broad assortment of applications and innovative ways of utilizing the technology for educational purposes in general.

Educational Newsgroups: Log onto the Internet and access your NewsWatcher (or any newsreader) so that you can subscribe to any of the following Newsgroups.

part **3**

k12.chat. teacher
k12.chat.elementary
k12.chat.junior
k12.chat.senior
k12.ed.special

Search Tools: Use one of the many Gopher browsing tools to initiate in-depth information searches. Many Gophers allow you to search not only text-based materials, but related picture, sound, and video material as well. With a Gopher you can both browse for information as well as download the information to your personal computer. Some Gophers will give you access to a host of archival information found on the Archie file. Gophers can also connect you to an assortment of electronic phone books for regions across the United States. Popular Gopher client software includes:

TurboGopher or TurboGopher VR (for Macs)
HGopher, WSGopher, or Chameleon (for Windows)

Special Web Pages: If exploring the Web, check out two informative educational arenas:

The K–12 Outpost: *http//k12.cnidr.org*
Apple's Educator Page: *http://www.info.apple.com.education*

ERIC Online: Many classroom teachers who are advancing their level of certification or who may be part of a graduate school program hail the ERIC database information system. This resource has been around for years, and just keeps getting better and better. The educational database was once available only via university library systems or intermediate school district library systems. It has been a frequently used source for securing educational research articles on large numbers of education-related topics. ERIC is now available on many Internet sites.

Let's Talk–Education: Live chat is one of the most popular applications of Internet technology to date. Live chat allows you to have on-line conversations with people around the world. Live chat is easy to access and use. Once on the Internet, you will find a vast array of live chat arenas. You should be aware that there are hundreds of live chat possibilities dedicated to any number of live chat topical themes. I've noted just one that might be of special interest to educators. It is easily accessible and easy to use, but only if you are an America Online subscriber.

part

3

■ America Online: Log on and opt for an *electronic conference room.* Using the keyword ESH, locate the *Electronic Schoolhouse.* Within the ESH is *the schoolroom,* where many teachers hang out. You can engage in live chat to talk about issues, concerns, or just to exchange ideas.

■ For those non-AOL users, several chat groups are available if you can access Telenet in order to connect with a computer using an IRC client. You made need a little advice from a "techie" for these groups, but if persistent you can find a way. Once you've connected to an IRC server, any of the following addresses will get you to a live chat education group.

csz.bu.edu	Massachusetts
irc.colorado.edu.	Colorado
irc.uiuc.edu	Illinois

Homework Help: Sometimes the questions that students have are not always going to arise during school hours. Wouldn't it be nice for students to have help available during evening hours when many are *doing* their homework? The Internet to the rescue! There are dozens of bulletin boards, chat rooms, and forums that give students the opportunity to ask for help with any number of school-related homework problems. Many of these services have *real teachers on-line* to answer student homework questions. Commercial service providers often recruit teachers to become on-line electronic tutors. Teachers are usually reimbursed for their time with free on-line time with the service provider. Because these tutors are real professionals, adults can worry less about the students who just want easy answers. On-line tutors will work through your students' questions, offering tips and explaining procedures—not just doling out answers. Below are listed a few of the places where homework help may be found.

- America Online: Academic Assistance Center. Search word—"homework". Live chat with real teachers between 5:00 pm and 1:00 am every day {EST}. In addition to this service, AOL provides a teacher paging service. Search word—"teacher pager". Type in your grade level, your question, and click *send.* E-mail answers are guaranteed within 48 hours. Homework help is also available for university students if your work is research-based. Once in the AAC, enter "research".
- Any Internet Source: Teacher paging on the Internet or with any CSP. Enter this address: homework24@aol.com.
- Compuserve: see the Student's Forum. Search word—"go stufo".
- GEnie: Access the Computer Assisted Learning Center. Homework questions are posted by subject. Real time chat is available Mondays and Wednesdays, 9:00 pm–10:00 pm (EST) & Tuesdays and Thursdays, 10:00–11:00 pm (EST).
- Prodigy: Access the Education Bulletin Board or Homework Helper. Helper is a premium service and an extra charge is assigned for services rendered.

part

3

Publications: Keep in mind that most commercial service providers have dozens of newspapers and magazines on-line. A few of these include *National Geographic, Newsweek, New York Times, Time Magazine, and U.S. News.*

Developing Your Lessons

The Internet can really work to a teacher's advantage as both an instructional and professional tool. Teaching can become easier and more rewarding as we add this tool to our already diverse assortment of educational tools. Like tools employed in any other instructional method, good teachers will thoughtfully plan for its introduction to the students. An Internet excursion should provide students with experiences that develop skills and encourage personal and academic growth. Teachers should avoid using this technological medium as a tool for free time entertainment or an inconsequential appendage to their curricular vision. It must become an integrated part of the educational process, enmeshed within the fabric of the curriculum.

Technology-Based Lesson Plans

Every educational application of Internet technology should begin with a good lesson plan. Minimally, this plan will consist of:

- two or more broad instructional goals
- a defined set of learner outcomes
- a description of materials required
- an outline describing instructional methods and procedures
- a listing of student activities and responsibilities
- an instructional time line
- a comprehensive assessment plan that identifies the procedures for evaluating student performances

Because your lesson plan is based on use of the Internet, the **broad goals** that you establish in your plan should focus on one or more of the following *information handling skills*. The Information Age skills that you are broadly addressing include:

1. Enabling students to "handle" large volumes of electronic information stores. The ability to determine what information is needed before going on-line so as not to become "lost" in a sea of information sources.

2. Developing skills which help students identify information that is essential and related to the task at hand. Information identification skills also include developing proficiencies which aid students in prioritizing and scaffolding information schemes. Helping students arrange information sources in increments of greater and lesser importance.

3. Developing information acquisition skills. After identifying relevant information, students must be competent in knowing how to acquire that information. In the least this should include an understanding of Web links and hypertext formats, printing hard copies of information, saving on-line files to disk, etc.

Learner outcomes should be more precise and serve as the culmination of specific performance objectives. Regardless of your topical plan (seeking information on Civil Rights, Insects, Weather, or Current Events . . .), *Information Age skills* that you should specifically regard include:

1. Information analysis—separating and dissecting information so that it may be studied, examined, and analyzed.

2. Information application—applying the information found in a search activity and relating that information to the task at hand. Putting the information to a purposeful use.

3. Self evaluation skills—encouraging students to consider the value of the information acquired. How well did all of the information sources "fit" together to complete a whole? How does the student feel on task completion? What is the student's reaction to the product of the lesson? Self-evaluation should include an examination of what went right and wrong within the learning process.

TBLPs and Assessment Issues

As teachers increase the number of technology-facilitated learning opportunities, we must not neglect important *assessment issues*. Applying Internet lesson plans in your classroom will require you to consider carefully how the fruit of student labor will be appraised.

Lesson plans that make use of Internet technology will require teachers to spend more time assessing thought and the products of thinking as opposed to assessing right and wrong responses to a conventional quiz or test instrument. Your assessments must involve the evaluation of student choices, decision-making skills, interpretive skills, analytical skills, and applied skills. The evaluation plan should define mechanisms for teacher evaluations of student competence and growth, *and* mechanisms that allow student self-examination.

For years teachers have been struggling to facilitate learning that transcends the mere knowledge level of Bloom's taxonomy. Internet plans can help teachers facilitate knowledge which requires higher-level thought. Assessing higher-level thought requires a scheme different from those used in assessing lower-level knowledge forms. One construct teachers have found especially adaptable to Internet lesson plans is the *performance-based assessment system.*

Performance-based assessments require learners to be submitted to a real world learning environment. The Internet fits that description nicely. It is a real world environment which will require students to perform in conditions that are filled with the interjections of other human and non-human information entities. Each exposure to a real world Internet experience requires the learner to perform in the midst of on-line interactions, commentary, discussion, and critique by a host of players.

It is common knowledge that teachers assess competence for two reasons. Frequent assessments contribute to increased learning and increased motivation. One might argue how quizzes or tests increase motivation, yet it is evident that for many students they really do! Consider how much more a performance based assessment system can enhance learning and motivation. Much of what we do in the pursuit of daily living requires real world, "on-the-job" performances. In many respects it is knowing that our performance is depended on that encourages us to do quality work. Knowing that performances are evaluated by external authorities motivates an individual to perform well and increases his or her efficiency. This type of reasoning can be present in any real world learning scenario.

Let's consider for a moment what constitutes a student performance so that we can better envision what a performance-based Internet plan might require.

1. Performances require preparation: The learner must prepare, practice, experiment and self-evaluate.

2. Performances are created: Learners must share an interpretive point of view.

3. Performances require performing: Learners are required to demonstrate competence before or amidst others.

4. Performances are interactive: There is a give and take between a number of participants.

5. Performances receive immediate feedback: Learners realize the impact of the actions in an immediate sense.

6. Performances are social: Learners gain satisfaction and input from an audience via conversation, interaction, appreciation, praise, and criticism.

7. Performances are judged: Others provide commentary on how to improve a performance.

8. Performances are qualitative: Success is measured by "degrees of quality" in the demonstration.

Performance-based education is not really a new phenomenon. However, it has been relegated to educational venues that have not always been academic. As the number of academic fairs, science fairs, and academic olympic events increases, we begin to see how performance-based assessments are beginning to catch on. Now that the Internet has arrived on the scene, teachers are afforded one more way to implement a performance-based learning opportunity.

part 3

Benefiting From Performance

The benefits of implementing performance-based assessment are many.

- The quality of content-related materials can be interpreted with greater accuracy. The product provides evidence of real world competency.
- The assessment is more holistic and comprehensive. Evaluations are not made from randomly sampled student responses.
- Students become part of the evaluation process and become self-invested in their work.
- The assessment may be multidimensional as the work requires a number of higher level cognitive capabilities.
- The assessment may more accurately define student strengths and weaknesses
- The assessment rewards innovation, creativity, and individuality.

Improving Instruction with TBLPs

Technology-based lesson plans which utilize Internet resources improve instruction in many ways.

1. Students on-line are *actively involved.* They are immersed in a system which requires attentiveness and interactivity. They are constantly making choices and decisions which result in immediate consequences. They are allowed to investigate information sources in a trial and error manner. They are free to reverse their tracks and head out in new directions. They pursue knowledge actively and personally.

2. Students on-line are able to see knowledge in *relational* ways. Information links are established for students so that they are better able to construct knowledge based on concepts that are connected.

3. On-line experiences effectively merge higher-level thinking and the application of basic skills. Basic skills are necessary in order to read and identify information sources. However, students are unable to make choices about information without engaging in higher-order thinking skills.

part
3

4. Students on-line have the opportunity to delve deeply into subjects and themes. The immense nature of the Internet allow endless opportunities for students to explore with a limitless capacity. Teachers are relieved of the burden of providing students with source materials. Time spent collecting library samples or establishing reserve stacks may be quickly replaced with time spent with students as they return from the search experiences. Both the student and the teacher's rate of productivity can increase because students have an endless stream of easily accessible subject materials.

5. Students are able to work both individually and in groups. When working independently, learners are afforded the luxury of establishing their own working pace. When reporting collectively, students benefit from sharing information and exchanging ideas and opinions.

Teachers will find that the Internet is a tremendous tool for on-line learning both inside and outside of the four walls of a conventional classroom. Recent advances in Internet connectivity are nothing short of spectacular. Yet the super-intelligent networks that are being created for government, business, industry, and education will dwarf what may currently amaze us with even faster and more colossal networking capabilities.

Because the technological disposition of our society is changing and evolving so rapidly, it is imperative that today's educator work hard to keep abreast of the advances that can impact educational practice in positive ways. Few teachers have had time to immerse themselves in the technological revolution, so don't feel isolated if you feel rather intimidated by the imposing arrival of technology in your district. My best advice is to begin with small steps. Learn how to use the new tools at your disposal, and accept the reality that education must constantly change in both its physical and methodological constructs.

Internet technologies easily allow us to go beyond the four walls of our classrooms. We limit the many opportunities students have today if we perceive education as something that is only accomplished within conventional classroom settings (see the short story at the end of this chapter). Today, *the world can be your classroom!* The variety of experiences available to students and teachers should provoke us to tap into the new resources in conjunction with our buildings, books, and bulletin boards.

part

3

On-Line Learning

Today's teachers have at their disposal more educational tools than ever before. When we think about new learning technologies and the ability to use the Internet as an information highway, we are wise to keep in mind one thing: They are tools. Technology has provided us with these additional tools to use in harmony with the many other tools that are at an educator's disposal. The tool in and of itself is only as good as the teacher who puts the tool to good use.

To make Internet technologies work effectively, it is prudent for teachers to understand the role of information and instruction in today's world. *Technological literacy* is a term which refers to the extent to which people are aware of the role technology plays in the distribution, acquisition, and synthesis of information. Upon entering the world of the Internet, teachers are immediately confronted with the vast information stores available. It is easy to ask yourself this question: Now that I have access to all this stuff, what do I do with it?

The quantity of information currently available is influencing learning in profound ways. Teachers must innovate creative ways to establish new relationships amidst knowledge bases. In this regard, the Internet can be very helpful in presenting to students real world examples of *integrated knowledge*. Knowledge on the Net is organized in numerous ways, but it is typically presented in a relational way, or in accordance to related fields. Web-constructed hypertext allows students to see the connections between knowledge fields, and allows them the opportunity to pursue knowledge not in a linear or chronological way (the way most books do), but in a relational way.

Much of the information on the Internet is also *real world knowledge*. It is knowledge related to human interests and endeavors. It is knowledge that continually expands with individual input. It is knowledge that is gradually constructed. It is knowledge which can be interacted with, manipulated, added to, or subtracted from. At its best it is a "living" body of knowledge.

Teachers who encourage their students to work cooperatively in small groups will find that the Internet really does promote *collaborative learning*. The mere fact that the Internet is so vast may encourage students to do team information searches. When returning to combine information sources, it is unlikely that any two students will have accessed the same material or will have summarized or interpreted the data in the same way. This will provoke great discussion. As your students condense all of the information in preparation for sharing a group presentation, they will be reminded that some information is more important than other information. Students will intuitively establish a type of knowledge scaffold, which will prioritize information gleaned from the Net.

As educators we must realize that we cannot efficiently teach all of the information that currently makes up the world's knowledge base. In fact, it is not only impossible, but imprudent to consider the collecting and depositing of knowledge as the essence of education. Teachers who use the Internet in their classrooms should not be controlled and overwhelmed by the information available. Quite the contrary. Teachers need to use the Internet as a vehicle which gives control over information. Internet technologies provide a means by which students are able to *construct* knowledge schemes through individual searches, group dialogues, and guided instruction. I often refer to this type of learning as *architectural learning*. Students on-line are equipped with the ability to interrelate and manipulate knowledge fields. They are offered opportunities to modify concepts in order to arrive at predetermined learning outcomes.

part

3

On-line learning requires each of us to keep in mind that information is structured quite differently than what we may be used to. Conventional instruction attempts to create linkages between prior knowledge which exists within a student's field of experience and new knowledge which may extend beyond a student's field of experience. The linkages are often created in steplike fashion. They are also frequently linked in a chronological and conceptually sequential manner. Conventional teaching supplements (trade books, video, slides, etc.) are likewise contrived in rather linear ways. Teachers and students are comfortable with exposure to information that is presented in these types of expository or narrative formats.

Many on-line learning experiences expose us to information presented in radically different ways. The World Wide Web requires us to process information presented via multimedia and hypermedia formats. Multimedia has been defined as information presented in any given combination of text, graphic, animation, or video source, delivered via a computer host. *Hypermedia* combines multimedia with some form of program which allows for greater interactivity between the user, the software, and the hardware. Hypermedia allows audio and visual information to be linked together in ways that allow a user to navigate through layers of related information.

part
3

Because information in hypermedia is presented associatively (linking related concepts together) and not in linear or chronological ways, hypermedia seems especially conducive as a tool to facilitate learning in our students. Many have found that the creation of layered information stacks through hypermedia replicates the way in which concepts are formed in the human mind, linked together, built on, and expanded—based on prior knowledge and association.

Each student brings to the learning experience a highly individual domain of prior knowledge and experience. Learners draw different associations between new and former knowledge deposits. Hypermedia may become the ideal medium for both the delivery of new information *and* the synthesis and manipulation of previously acquired information. Hypermedia should not be recognized simply as an information conduit which mainlines information between a source and receiver. Rather, hypermedia might be considered an external pool of *schemata,* or schemes.

Schemes are considered internal mental structures by which individuals organize their environment. As learning occurs, knowledge schemes are modified or changed as information is identified, processed, and stored. Hypermedia becomes an *external* pool of knowledge concepts through which learners are challenged to make new associations.

External Internet information sources become audio and visual categories from which individuals can internally classify and store specific information and experiences.

Internet lesson plans can establish a *relationship* between external and internal schemes. The associations in the external pool are manipulated in much the same way knowledge associations are made within the internal cognitive structure of the learner. Learning with hypermedia is an exercise in *associative learning,* a fundamental principal of schema theory. It is consistent with what we know about the ways in which humans process and organize information.

Learning with hypermedia may be disorienting for the adult only because adults have become accustomed to narrative and expository knowledge bases which are conceptually sequential and often linear. Children have fewer years invested in the accumulation of linear knowledge and more readily invest themselves in opportunities with hypermedia. They have also become accustomed to the the structure of hypermedia presentation through many of their electronic entertainment games devices.

part

3

Hypermedia allows learners to interact with concrete audio, visual, pictorial, and graphic experiences. As they interact with new information they are allowed *control* over the manner in which information is linked, arranged, or ordered so that learners can most efficiently integrate prior knowledge experiences with new information. Hypermedia is especially effective for bridging concrete information and abstractions. Hypermedia also brings a certain realism to the lesson. Learners are often more receptive and willing to respond and perform the tasks before them.

With conventional instruction, serious consideration must be given whenever teachers attempt to incorporate "real world" supplements to text-based instruction. Going to a museum, watching a video, or interpreting abstractions with conventional instructional tools have to be planned in very concise ways. The time and planning required for each is often less than practical. Because most instructors find themselves short on time (and/or resources, transportation, etc.), teachers find that the greatest amount of information can be presented in the least amount of time by using linear, sequential, and chronological printed or aural materials. This accounts for a preponderance of print-delivered information and direct teaching activities. Issues of time management and limited resources usurp the implementation of many of our best interpretations and applications of contemporary learning theory.

However, Internet technologies in association with hypermedia now afford teachers and students real world experiences in ways that are personally attractive, meaningful, and practical.

Hypertext is the term used for text that does not exist on printed pages, but instead exists within a hypermedia program in the mind of your computer. Hypertext is indeed different from printed text in that printed text is static and of a permanent nature. Hypertext provides users with greater flexibility than conventional text. Words, paragraphs, and ideas can be linked together in conceptual ways without necessarily being sequential or linear. Hypertext is often characterized as being intuitive because users are provided the freedom to electronically search their text, locate key words or phrases, or cross-reference words and phrases with other words and phrases.

Hypertext allows a user to identify certain words and transform them into *active* words. When the word is clicked on—much the same ways users may click on a button—a sound or video clip related to the word can be immediately provoked into play. Thus, hypertext allows the user not only to cross link words to other words, but words to associated images, sounds, and video motion. Multimedia is elevated to hypermedia when hypertext is employed. As established earlier, the key element in hypermedia is the linking of information in a conceptual way so that users may navigate through the content in an associative, nonlinear style.

Two frequently used terms in the world of hypertext are *link* and *node*. Links are those connections between the conceptual elements of a project, while nodes contain text, images, or other related information within your information base. A link is essentially a navigation pathway, while a node incorporates any of your content elements, be they text, images, sound bytes, or documents. The key to effective association in hypermedia is the ways in which nodes and links are related. The associations must be logical and make sense to users.

Why Students Respond to Learning On-line

Educators have before them a multitude of goals and responsibilities. Among the most important of the responsibilities that a teacher may have is allowing each child to rise to his or her highest individual intellectual potential. In order to accomplish this goal we must examine what kinds of experiences children are having as they interface with our educational system. What are students' general attitudes toward school, specific subjects, and their own self-concepts?

part

3

Talk to experienced teachers and they will not find this surprising. Teachers have long maintained that the two biggest challenges facing the profession today are classroom management issues and keeping students motivated to learn. Substantial drops in student motivation, curiosity, and enthusiasm as they relate to school and grade-related changes are unsettling. The most dramatic decreases are found as children leave preschool and kindergarten and experience grade one. Further decreases are found as children exit primary school and enter middle school. It seems the older children get the more negatively they perceive themselves and the more pessimistic they feel about schooling.

Preschoolers find frequent and immediate success in many of the tasks designed for them. Older primary children have fewer tasks designed to guarantee success, and frequently are subjected to instructional material that they are not ready for. This sets many children up for a failing precedent, spiraling them toward an inevitable state of learned helplessness. Students entering middle school confront major shifts in teaching methodology from earlier grades. The atmosphere for many students becomes competitive. Students may sense they are being addressed in a collective manner that is much less personal than former instructional styles. Likewise, assessment and grading schemes become more structured. How can teachers optimize student motivation in the midst of such realities?

Many educators have discovered that providing students with access to new learning technologies does wonders for classroom motivation. While it is true that motivation is more easily stimulated than maintained, there seems to be little doubt that students in general *love* technology.

Why is it that students seem to have such affection for a medium that many adults find intimidating and confusing? Perhaps one reason lies in the reality that children have grown up with technology. It has always been a part of of their experience. Preschoolers see a computer as an extended TV. It gives them pleasure, entertainment, and information. As children grow older they rely on technology for their music, their games, and as an aid to their studies.

As technology relates to a learner's academic studies, it is interesting to consider a few of the many possible reasons why on-line learning has become so very appealing.

1. Internet technology may increase the amount of **attention** students direct toward a learning task. Attention is a required condition for motivation simply because learners must attend to instructional ele-

ments in order to gain mastery over various instructional goals and objectives. Like motivation, gaining a learner's attention is much easier than sustaining it. Attention span is largely dominated by developmental constraints and teachers realize quickly that in order to sustain attention children must be actively involved in the learning processes. Frustrated by trying to design daily activities that actively engage students in every subject every day, many teachers begin to rely on paper and pencil activities that occupy students with busy work so that teachers can keep up with the demands of lesson planning, evaluation, and report making. As easy as it is to criticize what appears to be an easy way out, dittos and conventional assignments are often used as survival mechanisms for teachers who have too much to do and too little time to do it. On-line learning allows teachers to engage their students in active and constructive learning while simultaneously increasing professional opportunities to conference with their students and evaluate them in meaningful ways. Furthermore, attention is increased by the number of *sensory modalities* stimulated by Internet access. The presence of text, graphics, pictorial, and audio information presented in simultaneous contexts assists in maintaining student attention.

part

3

2. Internet technology may increase the degree to which learners perceive information to be **relevant**. Relevance suggests that learners perceive the content of the material they are interacting with is both substantive and important enough to warrant attention and manipulation. The information age has resulted in a deluge of transitory data and a colossal repository of factual information. Conventional instruction has attempted to integrate such information within a learner's life experience through memorization and recall. Because the amount of information has increased so dramatically in our society, education has tried to play catch up by having students process more and more data. Meanwhile the amount of time spent analyzing, discussing, and exploring the implications of new information in conventional classrooms have received less attention.

On-line learning requires students to synthesize data into meaningful and useful applications. TBLPs allow students to exchange novel ideas and indulge in academic exchanges in personalized ways. By so doing the information becomes useful and relevant as opposed to being sifted through a maze of contests which promotes academic trivia and objective quizzes. Internet technology can help learners integrate information in more meaningful contexts. It allows learners to search and select data on any given topic. It provides them with opportunities to invest themselves in the pursuit of knowledge, the presentation of knowledge, and an evaluation of the experience as a whole.

3. On-line learning increases a student's sense of **competence and control** over learning activities. When students believe that they can perform competently in school, they exhibit high levels of confidence. Learners are motivated when they perceive themselves as successful. Success becomes a predictor for future successes, as confidence breeds increased confidence. Unfortunately many conventional school assignments have not nurtured confidence or control in student life. When learners loose control of their own learning and become directed by others who might undermine student autonomy and confidence, it is reasonable to expect that students will be amotivated and troublesome. On-line learning becomes a means by which classrooms can be restructured so that teachers and students are placed in a win/win situation. Learners regain varying degrees of control and regulation while teachers are provided with greater instructional opportunities.

4. On-line learning increases levels of student **satisfaction** in learning. Learners are satisfied when they have fulfilled a need to achieve. The need to achieve can be based on internal or external elements. Internet TBLPs may be designed so that learners work toward inner satisfaction and are less concerned about the need to achieve based on social comparisons and teacher expectations. As much as we must orient children to have their own needs met, so too must teachers work to have their own needs met. Teachers who bask in the satisfaction that children are "working for them" may need to reevaluate the context of their professional aspirations. It is far better for students to be working for themselves than it is for them to be working for the teacher. Children often exhibit needs for approval in a variety of ways and degrees. Technology does not usurp the approval children may receive from teachers or peers. It does help to define the locus of satisfaction for a learner, however, so that "approval" becomes something of more permanent value.

part
3

Consider the Future

The following story has been designed as a vehicle to prompt thoughtful reflection about the future of technology in education. As you apply technology-based lesson plans in your classrooms, you will quickly observe how rapidly technology advances. As you read, consider this story as a futuristic illustration to think about critically. There are elements in the story that may be interpreted as positive statements regarding the future of technology in education. Other elements in the story may serve as cautionary statements about potential uses and abuses of technology in education. After you have read the story, take a moment and consider the best and worst features of this futuristic classroom. Summarize your reactions and consider responding to the story by sending me a note via Internet E-mail. My address is listed in the opening pages of this Guide.

The Virtual Classroom

A Short Story by Joseph Rivard

It was 7:00 am when the voice-activated alarm awoke thirteen-year-old Chris from a very deep sleep. It was Monday morning and the sound of his Mother's voice electronically duplicated by his alarm brought him little comfort as he realized the weekend was over and it was back to school today. Crawling slowly out of bed he slipped on a robe and went downstairs to get some breakfast. With his Dad out of town on business and his Mom having already gone out for the day, he sleepily consumed his favorite cereal, sipped his orange juice, and read a short note left by his mother. He was bored by the predictability of the script. A list of after school chores to be done and several options suggested for his dinner. Given some money left on the table and the invitation to eat out with his best friend, he ignored any other possibilities and was gladdened by the thought of having some social time at the end of such a foreboding Monday morning. Chris was hardly enamored with school, and while he had long since resigned himself to its inevitability, he didn't pretend to look forward to the way it drained his emotions and taxed his mind. He always returned so exhausted . . .

As Chris finished his breakfast he began to feel himself lose the morning groggies, and knew that a shower would really bring him up to speed. Double stepping the stairs he was quickly back in his room. The clock announced the time quarterly, and Chris realized that somewhere he had lost twenty minutes. The shower had best be a quick one, and as he stepped into the steamy stall he savored the feel of the hot water on his skin. If only he could spend today outdoors. Chris loved the feel of natural elements against his flesh. Wind, rain, sun . . . it didn't matter. As long as it was real.

Climbing out of the shower, Chris surveyed the condition of his room. A twelve-by-fourteen state of confusion. The closet door stared gapingly open before him revealing an unprecedented amount of clutter within. With dirty clothes piled high in one corner and magazines scattered recklessly around the floor he sensed it was time to clean things up a bit. This thought was prompted not merely because of some intrinsic sense of responsibility, but because his dad was due home Wednesday. Against the wall on his right stood his ever-faithful entertainment system. Chris remained impressed with it massiveness, especially since he had invested years of birthday money and Christmas requests in the construction of the electronic marvel. Yet there was neither time to clean or be entertained, he thought, as he slowly glanced to his left. It was time to begin.

Standing conspicuously against the north wall of the room was a small booth. Hanging coldly above the door of the booth was a school uniform. He often called it his diving suit, as it reminded him of the scuba gear divers wore back around 2010. He finished drying himself, dropping his bath towel carelessly on the floor. He reached for his uniform slowly. As he stepped into it he could feel the rubbery insulation press clammily against his skin. He hated the sensation. It was like putting on a wet bathing suit after you had dried off. He knew that for the next several hours his body was destined to be confined within this synthetic cocoon. Once on-line, he knew the uniform would become like a second skin, but for the moment he felt as if every pore was suffocating.

Chris dreaded the preliminaries involved in school engagement. He quickly secured his uniform and began a brief systems check. It was essential that the numerous fiber optic cables embedded within the Lycra suit function without flaw. Likewise, the umbilical cord connecting his uniform to his in-house computing booth must be secured. Having made the necessary connections, Chris was ready to go on-line. He stepped inside the booth and secured the door. The interior of the booth was rather stark. The small walled environment was embellished with a myriad of small screens, LED indicator lights, cameras, microphones, speakers, sensors, and eyeware. Chris could stand or sit with ease, and the reclining cushioned chair seemed the one luxury the booth contained. Encased in blackness, Chris punched the glowing green button marked "school engagement." On a screen to his right Chris relaxed as he witnessed the system conduct an additional computerized self check on all systems. Only a moment or two passed when the screen confirmed that Chris was indeed on-line with all systems fully functioning.

Starville Public Schools required a rather precocious log on procedure. On a small monitor labeled "Starville," the system asked Chris to first enter his student ID code. The code was numeric, so he entered his number using a small digital keypad located below the monitor. A small digital clock now displayed real time flashing slowly on the Starville monitor. Fortunately Chris had logged in on time. He couldn't afford another tardy notice, for his parents had warned him that if he was late for school engagement one more time, he would not be able to play CyberTrek with Eming. Such deprivation would be difficult to take, as Chris had found Eming to be an auspicious competitor in the sport. Locally, most of his friends in the neighborhood seemed to have very predictable playing strategies. International competitors like Eming were savored. Her approach to the game was so unlike his own.

Placing his forehead close against an upholstered brace, Chris sat motionless as a laser passed quickly across his right retina. In addition to a retinal scan, Chris was required to submit a hand imprint on a touch screen to his left, and speak his name for voice recognition by the Starville security system. Finally with his attendance confirmed, Chris was able to access his school dayplan. Speaking clearly into a small microphone, Chris instructed the system.

part

3

> *"Retrieve Dayplan—October 17, 2077 AM*
> *Starville PS #107—Instructor: Ms. J. Jenkins*
> *Level 8 Student—Christian Weiss."*

Chris soon heard the prerecorded voice of Ms. Jenkins welcoming him to the new day's adventure. The general direction contained within each day plan was hardly surprising to Chris, as he and Ms. Jenkins mapped out his academic direction mutually. While the state mandated various aspects of the level eight curricula, a great deal of what was accomplished was at the discretion of Ms. Jenkins and Chris. Starville was proud of the fact that none of its students failed the basic competence required by exiting assessments, and Chris knew that the basic level eight academic skills were hardly challenging. What worried Chris was not the exit exams for level eight. What worried Chris was whether or not he was prepared to handle the problem-solving simulations developed by the Starville Life Skills System. Life skills simulations were designed to assess problem-solving abilities, and students were individually evaluated for competency in that area. While Chris had selected various areas of academic interest and extra curricular enrichment, he never knew how Ms. Jenkins and the SLS system would use those topics as a vehicle to teach problem-solving and life skills.

Glancing at the dayplan, the suspicion that Chris had was confirmed. There were no skills-based lessons offered this morning, and the system informed him that he had the option to engage in an SLS system enactment given one of the following broad contexts.

(1) History—Events leading to World War III

(2) Science—Research History: The Cancer Cure

(3) Art History—1990–2000

(4) Enrichment—Terrestrial Vehicles/ Early Porsche Sport Automobiles

part

3

Chris knew all too well that the options before him were optional only in sequence. What he did not select first would unavoidably return on a future menu to haunt him later in the day or sometime in the future on another dayplan. Nevertheless, Chris was not one to put off pleasure, so he opted for enrichment. He had often shared his passion for terrestrial transportation with Ms. Jenkins, especially his affinity for Porsche sporting land vehicles popular between 1950–1999. Having selected item four, an extensive menu regarding vehicle selection succeeded. Chris was able to select a car of choice (make, model, year), various automotive options, and even his favorite color. Chris opted for a black 1979 Porsche 928S. Selecting choices from the menu was simple enough, but Chris realized that the core experiences the SLS system would contrive for him would be much more complex. Using information previously programmed by Ms. Jenkins and SLS consultants, he suspected that the life skills adventure ahead of him would hardly be so elementary.

The Starville monitor marked briefly real time once again before a viewing field was lowered from the top of the booth over his head. It was black and silent. Suddenly there appeared a door. He knew that beyond the door was an alternate reality. A reality contrived by SLS. A reality conjured up by information sources outside himself, and responsive to whatever words and actions he would initiate from this point forward. He hesitated before opening the door, realizing that once he stepped into the virtual field he was committed to the conclusion of the exercise. He would be immersed within a world outside of real time and space. With his heart pounding and his muscles tightening he reached for the door.

Weeks earlier Ms. Jenkins had met with SLS technician programmers (often referred to as "RCs"). RCs were "reality creators," and it was an RC's task to work with professional educators in creating life experiences in an alternate reality. The realities created by the RCs were diverse in nature. The desired outcomes from each experience varied, as there were reality experiences for each of the major academic disciplines per student level. There were also thematic realities which coalesced a number of disciplines in order to perpetuate an interdisciplinary educational approach. There were realities for the arts, and realities for sports and physical fitness. Each of these realities allowed for technical modification by those at SLS, as well as individual student interactivity. The core paths within each primary reality construct were preauthored and distributed by satellite by the National Education Institute. Starville received transmissions at will from this education utility as did thousands of other localized educational sectors.

part

3

While the RCs loved to modify the base realities conjured by NEI, there was no greater pleasure for them than the opportunity to fashion individual student enrichment realities. Local RCs had complete autonomy and freedom of design in the creation of the enrichment realities. They worked only with the student's teacher, but were required by law to be licensed for reality creation.

Ms. Jenkins was concise and explicit in the description of what she had in mind. She wanted to provide student Christian Weiss with a life experience exploring the dangers of substance abuse. She was aware of Christian's affinity for 1900's terrestrial sports cars, and believed that a scenario involving drinking and driving might be an effective way to present the dangers involved in the digestion of unauthorized chemical substances. The reality should depict an accurate rendering of the implications of drinking and driving as it would relate to whatever context Chris might select.

Obtaining information regarding the various makes and models of the Porsche was easily accomplished by accessing one of several automotive hobby databases. Hundreds of minute details for each model were fed into the SLS system. Regardless of the Porsche that Chris might select, SLS could translate the information into a virtual vehicle capable of being virtually driven down any number of roads and highways defined by script. Ms. Jenkins had determined that she would invite Mr. and Mrs. Weiss to meet Chris within the reality as a part of the life experience. The experience would begin with a birthday party at Christian's house celebrating his sixteenth birthday. His Mom and Dad would then take him out to the garage and hand him a set of keys. Upon opening the garage door Chris would find the Porsche of his dreams. Present would also be Christian's best friend. Together they would be encouraged to take the car out for a drive. Christian's best friend would be a virtual construction however, preprogrammed to initiate a series of events within the reality. Among other things, he would encourage Chris to pick up some alcohol so that they could really celebrate the occasion of his birthday. There were any number of choices Chris could make throughout the experience, but the SLS technicians were reasonably certain that the combined enticements of both speed and alcohol would cooperate to create at least one "worse case" scenario. Given the geographic parameters of the script it was likely that if all the *wrong* choices were made, Chris would end up southbound on Michigan Interstate 75 at the M59 west exit ramp. There, Chris and his best friend would lose control of the vehicle being driven as they were trying to maneuver a sharp curve rising abruptly from the exit ramp. Of course that was a worst case scenario. With each RC having a bit of Hollywood within, they looked forward to creating a number of different dramas capable of occurring, depending on the choices Chris would make within his virtual life experience.

It was a perfect night. Chris couldn't believe he was actually at the wheel of this ebony angel. The 4664 cc engine sang as it cut through the night. The stereo pumped energy into the cockpit as his best friend urged Chris to open it up a bit as they cruised the last few miles of the expressway before reaching home. Chris punched the accelerator and could feel the strength of 300bhp pushing him back into the leather bucket. The 928's 0.38 drag coefficient allowed the phantom to slice through the darkness as Chris glanced at the speedometer. Eighty five, ninety, one hundred miles an hour. What a car! Strong and stable, there was little to prove their speed nary the speedometer and the rate at which the highway lampposts disappeared in succession.

Chris was driven by the speed, and fueled by a subtle arrogance from the few drinks he had consumed earlier. He was enjoying just a slight buzz. A bit light-headed, happy, and confident, Chris pursued the challenge prompted by his friend. Faster . . . faster. One hundred and ten, one hundred and twenty, one hundred and thirty. Chris could feel every sensation, every vibration. Every sound made him feel so alive, every image pressed brilliantly in his memory. He was excited, enticed, and enamored. Still he was twenty-five mph short of the 928's capable top speed. Chris pulled his foot from the accelerator, deciding to save something for the next time out. As he did so he realized he was nearly on top of the M59 exit ramp. Chris braked hard and heard rubber tearing from the concrete. His heart was pounding, his blood pressure rising. The 928 never made the curve. It was a one hundred and five mile an hour projectile hurtling over the embankment. Chris could feel himself floating in midair. It was if he were moving in slow motion. He looked to his right and saw the terror across his friend's face. He heard the scream of shearing metal and the shatter of glass. He felt the crash and experienced some tremendous pressure against his chest. He heard his friend scream as he realized the car roof was caving in. Terror consumed him as darkness tore the light from his eyes and engulfed him.

The SLS technicians monitored Christian's heartbeat and blood pressure carefully. It was silent within the booth now, with only the heavy breathing of the displaced thirteen-year-old audible to the RCs. They were quite pleased. The reality they had contrived for Chris worked flawlessly. It was standard operating procedure to allow the subject some quiet time prior to establishing real time audio or visual communication. Chris would need a little orientation time prior to completing the debriefing which succeeded each life skills experience. It was Chris who initiated real time communication first. He was reporting VIM sickness. Visually induced motion sickness was common for reality experiences such as the one Chris had just completed. Immersed within his three-dimensional reality, Chris was exposed to numerous visual, aural, and haptic cues during his experience. However, the absence of movement cues from within his body caused him to become disoriented.

part 3

Chris made it out of the booth and into the bathroom just in time. The nausea was overwhelming and his favorite morning cereal reappeared in the midday vomit. It was now lunchtime, but he had little desire to try to eat again. He could join some of his friends in one of their favorite virtual games, but for the moment seemed simply content to rest. He opened his bedroom window and felt a cool breeze sweep softly against his skin. Back in real time . . . it felt good. Suddenly he felt the need to see his best friend. His death seemed so authentic. Memories flooded his mind as the life experience recreated itself in his thoughts. Interrupted by his beeping pager, Chris realized it was time to re-engage. As he walked wearily toward the booth he wondered what Ms. Jenkins had in store for him this afternoon.

Glossary

AltaVista
A popular search engine for the World Wide Web.

Archie
An Internet service that maintains and catalogs information stored on anonymous ftp sites worldwide.

ASCII
American Standard Code for Information Interchange; the computer codes for the 128 text-only (numbers, punctuation marks, upper- and lower-case letters) characters.

attachment
A binary file attached to a mail message for sending over the Internet.

bandwidth
A metaphorical term for how much information can flow through a specified point at any given time.

BBS
Bulletin Board System; A computer system that provides its users downloadable files and discussion areas.

Binary
A type of computer file that contains non-text data; may not be sent over the Internet without conversion.

Binhex
A common type of routine on Macintosh computers for converting binary files to text for Internet transmission.

BITNET
An early supernetwork of academic computers; now mostly encompassed by the Internet.

browser
A computer program that allows you to access and navigate the contents of the World Wide Web, either by clicking the mouse or pressing certain keys. Examples are Netscape, Cyberdog, and Internet Explorer.

client
The program or computer that interacts with a server.

command line
A type of system that requires you to type in commands to the computer to operate it; also called a shell account or a Command Line User Interface (CLUI); contrasted with Graphical User Interface such as the Macintosh or Windows.

compress
To make a file smaller before transferring over the Internet to save time and bandwidth.

cross post
Simultaneously send a message to more than one *newsgroup*.

dialup
A type of computer connection to a network which uses a modem and telephone lines.

digest
A compilation of several messages posted to an Internet *newsgroup*, sent to subscribers as a single message.

DNS

(Domain Name Server) The computer that knows the addresses of all the other computers on the Internet.

download

To get or retrieve a file from another computer.

E-mail

Electronic mail of messages sent via the Internet.

emoticons

The combination of punctuation marks that, when viewed sideways, resembles a facial expression that is lost in text-based communication. For example,:-) is a smile used to indicate "I'm just joking."

emulator

Software that allows one computer to act like another one, usually a VAX VT-100, the standard Internet terminal.

FAQ

Frequently Asked Questions; lists of questions that seem to appear over and over again on BBSs, Usenet groups, etc.; compiled and regularly reposted in order to cut down on the number of newby questions.

flame

A rude or derogatory message directed as a personal attack against an individual or group.

flame war

A nasty, often vulgar, exchange of insults over the Internet.

ftp

File Transfer Protocol. A method of transferring data over the Internet.

GIF

A standard format of compressing and converting to ascii graphic information (i.e., pictures). Files with names ending in ".gif" are GIF files. The most common format for transferring graphical information over the Internet.

Gopher
A menu driven system of sending files to and from other computers on the Internet. Predecessor to the World Wide Web.

header
The mass of techical gobbledygook at the top of E-mail or Usenet messages.

home page
A page on the World Wide Web that acts as a starting point for information about a person or organization.

hypertext
Text that contains embedded *links* to other pages of text. Hypertext enables the reader to navigate between pages of related information by following links in the text.

html
Hypertext Markup Language; the standard set of codes (or "tags") inserted into a document to make it usable over the World Wide Web.

http
Hypertext Transport Protocol; the language World Wide Web computers use to communicate with each other.

IP
Internet Protocol; the standard language Internet computers use to talk to each other.

IP Number
The unique numeric address assigned to every computer on the ternet.

IRC
Internet Relay Chat. Live, keyboard to keyboard E-mail discussions

home page
The starting point for a World Wide Web site; the first page you see at a site.

host
The computer you connect to when you want to access the Internet.

hypertext
Specially-coded text which comprises the language of the World Wide Web.

ISP
Internet Service Provider; where you get your access to the Internet.

kermit
A method of transferring files from one computer to another; named after a small green animal which can transfer information faster than kermit can.

keyword
A descriptive term you enter into a search engine to try to find information; similar to Yellow Pages headings, for example.

link
A reference to a location on the Web that is embedded in the text of Web page. Links are usually highlighted with a different color or underline to make them easily visible.

list
A mechanism for automatically sending *E-mail* messages to a group of subscribers.

Listserv
Proper name for a type of software program that automatically handles the work associated with mailing lists, such as distributing mail to all subscribers. Occasionally used to refer to a mailing list itself. Other similar programs are LISTPROC and MAJORDOMO.

listserver
Common name for a Listserv type program that manages a *list*.

login
Identifying yourself with your user I. D. and password to a host computer.

lurk
To read the messages on a LISTSERV or Usenet group without contributing.

lurker
A passive reader of an Internet *newsgroup*. A lurker reads messages, but does not participate in the discussion by posting or responding to messages.

modem
Short for modulate / demodulate, a device which allows your computer to speak to other computers via telephone lines.

MOO
MUD, Object Oriented. A type of MUD (see below) which allows for meaningful objects to be placed in the room.

Mosaic
An aging browser for the World Wide Web.

MPEG
Motion Pictures Expert Group; a file format for compressing video.

MUD
Multiple User Domain. A place ("room") on the Internet where live, on-line "chats" occur.

Netiquette
Good manners ('net etiquette). Appropriate behavior when communicating with other people you don't know over the Internet. E.g., not typing in all capital letters: IT MEANS YOU'RE SHOUTING!!!

Netscape
The most popular browser ("client") for the World Wide Web; others are Mosaic, Microsoft Internet Explorer, and Cyberdog.

newbie
Slang for a new user of the Internet.

newsgroups
Global discussion groups posted on the Internet.

page
A single document, regardless of length, on a World Wide Web site.

post
To send a message or response to a Usenet newsgroup or LISTSERV.

PPP
Point to Point Protocol; a method of directly connecting one's desktop computer to the Internet. Similar to SLIP.

quoting
To reproduce a portion of a message (E-mail, newsgroup, LISTSERV) within the text of your reply so that readers know to what you are referring.

search engine
A program which will search the Internet for information you request. Popular ones are veronica (for Gopher) and AltaVista (for the World Wide Web).

server
A machine on a network that provides information and services to the client computers that are connected to it.

signature
Identifying lines added onto E-mail and Usenet messages you send, usually containing your name and E-mail address. Some may be elaborate. Best avoided.

SLIP
Serial Line Internet Protocol; similar to PPP but older, a method of directly connecting one's desktop computer to the Internet.

spam
To send the same obnoxious (or commercial) message to millions of people at once. Highly frowned on.

Spiders
Software programs that roam the Web collecting information for indexes.

TCP/IP
The combination of Transmission Control Protocol and Internet Protocol; the language that allows computers on the Internet to communicate with each other.

telnet
Allows you to remotely login and operate a remote computer with your own via the Internet

thread
A related group of Usenet messages, consisting of an original post and all the responses to it.

URL
Uniform Resource Locator: The notation for specifying Web page addresses (e.g., http://www.abacon.com).

USENET
The section of the Internet that is devoted to *newsgroups*.

userid
User I. D.; the name assigned to you for the purpose of logging in when you receive your Internet account.

uucode
Another standard, similar to Binhex, for converting binary files to ascii files for transmission over the Internet.

VT100
A very early model of terminal for connecting to Digital Computers; obsolete but their interface has become the standard.

WAIS
Wide Area Information Search. A tool for searching and receiving information on the Internet.

Winsock
A standard that Microsoft Windows programs use to interact with the Internet.

Veronica
The search engine for Gopher; allows users to search Gopherspace by typing in a number of keywords.

ZModem
Like XModem, YModem, and Kermit, a method for transferring data from one computer to another; ZModem is the most advanced, the quickest, and most reliable.